WHEN THE EARTH EXPLODES: VOLCANOES AND THE ENVIRONMENT

WHEN THE EARTH EXPLODES: VOLCANOES AND THE ENVIRONMENT

BUCK DAWSON

Kroshka Books
Commack, New York

Editorial Production: Susan Boriotti
Office Manager: Annette Hellinger
Graphics: Frank Grucci and John T'Lustachowski
Information Editor: Tatiana Shohov
Book Production: Donna Dennis, Patrick Davin, Christine Mathosian, Tammy Sauter and Diane Sharp
Circulation: Maryanne Schmidt
Marketing/Sales: Cathy DeGregory

Library of Congress Cataloging-in-Publication Data

Dawson, Buck.
　　When the earth explodes : volcanoes and the environment / by Buck Dawson.
　　　　p.　　　　cm.
　　ISBN 1-56072-450-1
　　1. Volcanoes.　2. Weather--Effect of volcanic eruptions on.　3. Archaeology and natural
disasters.　4. Volcanoes--Environmental aspects.　I. Title.
QE522.D29　　　　　　　　1997　　　　　　　　　　　　　97-36650
551.21—dc21　　　　　　　　　　　　　　　　　　　　　　CIP

Copyright © 1998 by　Buck Dawson
　　　Kroshka Books. A division of
　　　Nova Science Publishers, Inc.
　　　6080 Jericho Turnpike, Suite 207
　　　Commack, New York 11725
　　　Tele. 516-499-3103　　　　　Fax 516-499-3146
　　　e-mail: Novascience@earthlink.net
　　　e-mail: Novascil@aol.com
　　　Web Site: http://www.nexusworld.com/nova

Printed in the United States of America

to

Tommie Kirksmith, my volcano editor through several eruptions

John Bagby, the real scientist in our family who kept me honest during my agony
of unpopularity as an anti-establishment environmentalist

and

Colleen M. Wilson, my editorial assistant

CONTENTS

PREFACE

A Theory is a tool – not a creed – J.J. Thompson

Of all the sciences, geology should be the most physical. It is literally carved in stone and yet the theories on what makes volcanoes erupt are as hard to prove as any science fiction. We know what has happened in the past – when, where and how often – in the brief time span history represents. We know what boils out of volcanoes and that molten rock (magma) is the immediate underlying cause. Beyond that, it is at best educated guesswork. Who is to say that the current theories about plates moving back and forth underneath the earth's crust will hold up over the centuries and millenniums that volcanoes will continue to operate? We now explain "scientifically" what we once attributed to angry gods... but are we any closer to solving the riddle?

Volcanoes give life and take it away. Without them, there would be no water and no life, so they give or have given far more than they take away. Still, the results of eruptions are at least temporary disruptions more dramatic and catastrophic and unexplainable than anything known to man or any other form of life on Earth. I am not so much a volcanologist (the age old science of volcanoes) as I am a story teller fascinated with the history, the unpredictable but violent and exciting stories past, present and future that volcanoes play in our lives from famines, plagues and revolutions to the climate related problems we face today. The most fascinating element about volcanoes is their unleashed power about which we know so little. In a time when man has figured out most everything – or thinks he has – volcanoes remain a mystery that can strike any time and almost any place. Man in all his arrogance is no more capable of solving the riddle than were the all mighty dinosaurs before him.

– Buck Dawson

WHO IS THAT MASKED MAN WITH A PATCH?

Born on Halloween, 1920 in Orange, New Jersey, Buck's parents were spooked even before his pumpkin-shaped head and his eye patch became his regular "costume". Little did his parents know he'd "spook" the world with his crazy antics. You name it, Buck knows it. Whether it's camping, sports, food, politics or volcanoes. Wherever you go, people know him. Former U.S. Presidents, movie stars, Olympic greats, professors, scientists. Buck has made his mark on the world and continues to do so with gusto!

Raised in Easton, Penn., Buck went to prep school at Blair Academy (NJ) where he was an all-state track captain and a state champion halfback on their undefeated football team. His sports talent continued at the University of Michigan and included freshman football and running on the track team. He was a member of the Phi Gamma Delta fraternity. Despite the fact that it took him nine years to graduate (due to WWII), Buck was elected to Michigauma, the senior honor society. His writing career took off at Michigan where he won a Hopwood Prize. He has written hundreds of short stories and 19 books on subjects ranging from the Civil War to swimming. In fact, look for Dawson's newest release due out from Kroshka soon: *Those Million Dollar Mermaids: America's Love Affair With Its First Olympic Swimmers.*

Midway through Michigan, Dawson served in WWII as a combat infantry platoon leader in both the 10th Mountain Division and the 82nd Airborne. He also served as a ski-trooper and then as a much decorated glider-trooper fighting in Normandy, Holland, the Bulge and across the Rhine and the Elbe. In Berlin, he was the public information officer during initial occupation and also served as one of General Gavin's aides.

After making a movie with Marlene Dietrich and Billy Wilder and jumping off Hitler's balcony to impress Ingrid Bergman, Buck wrote the history of the 82nd Airborne--more than 15,000 copies have since been circulated and the book is in its third reprint. He was a writer for Admiral Carney at the start of NATO, stationed on the side of Mt. Vesuvius. In addition, he served as assistant to the director of the Peace Corps.

After his war service and directing the first women's swim camp (Ak-O-Mak) in Ontario, Canada inherited from his father-in-law, 1952 Olympic swim coach Matt Mann, Dawson was named chairman of the AAU Committee that first got the Swimming Hall of Fame off the ground. He later served as its first executive director for 25 years. He made Fort Lauderdale's International Swimming Hall of Fame grow from an idea -- to a shoe box collection to a multi million dollar operation as the showcase and archives for swimming, diving, water polo and synchronized swimming. He is also the founder and first president of the Association of Sports Museums and Halls of Fame -- a group of more than 140 Hall of Fame directors nationwide.

Dawson is hype, show business, collector, historian, dog trainer and fund raiser. But most of all, he has always gotten his kicks out of promoting something or somebody he believed in: General Ridgeway, General Gavin, the 82nd Airborne, Camps Ak-O-Mak and Chikopi, the University of Michigan, his wife, children, father-in-law, and ultimately the Hall of Fame, swimming and his books.

Dawson has completed five books in the past two years; *Stand Up and Hook Up* (Eakin Press) drew rave reviews from military circles and testimonials from Presidents Ford, Reagan and Carter. *Gold Medal Pools* (Hoffman Publishing) features the world's most beautiful pools including the White House pool and many Hollywood celebrities' pools. *We Don't Sew Beads On Belts* (Hoffman) is a scrapbook of memories of Camps Chikopi and Ak-O-Mak since their start in 1920. *Civil War Etchings* was recently published by Dover.

Residing half the year in Fort Lauderdale, the other in the Northwoods of Canada at his camp, Dawson has been honored as Distinguished Citizen of the Year, is a Commodore and a Golden Whale, and honor given by the American Red Cross' Longfellow Society. He has been the recipient of the R. Max Ritter Award, the highest honor bestowed by United States Swimming, and the W.R. Bill Schroeder Award, the most prestigious award from the Association of Sports Museums and Halls of Fame. He is known notoriously as "The Buck Never Stops"-- and was recently featured in an AMC (American Movie Classics) movie on the late Marlene Dietrich.

INTRODUCTION

Dawson's study of the environment began as a teenager sitting at his father's dinner table. His father was national president of Keep America Beautiful, our first significant environmental organization. Dawson's interest in volcanoes began in 1952 when he was stationed on the side of Mt. Vesuvius as a NATO Staff Officer in Naples, Italy. This book brings the two (environment and volcanology) together in a hard fact thesis that has been brewing in Dawson's mind for years.

The well documented science of volcanology is based on evidence gleaned from the great eruptions of the past 200 years. It proves that volcanoes are the only significant source of global air pollution.

Going backward from the medium sized eruptions of Pinatubo 1991 in the Philippines and El Chichõn 1981 in Mexico, Dawson tells his story of how volcanoes and NOT man burning fossil fuels causes global air pollution. His chapter of Pinatubo is from the eyewitness account from his nephew, the U.S. Navy Supply Officer stationed at Subic Bay.

He shows by volcano studies and graphs that for over 200 years that 95% of global air pollution has come from volcanoes, that there has been NO global warming trend over the last 200 years. He also defines the ozone (what it is and does, and explains the hole in the ozone and how it works). He describes "the Greenhouse Effect" as over rated and tells what really occurs that could or could not cause future problems with global warming.

Part II of this book covers the seven most significant eruptions in recorded history and graphically illustrates (often with eyewitness narrative) the awesome power of a single volcano and the ridiculous notion of man trying to control it.

Santorin	1500 BC	Set Western Civilization back 1200 years
Vesuvius	79 AD	Executioner of Pompeii
Laki	1783	Skaptor Jokel, Iceland and the Plague
Tambora	1815	50 cubic miles of dust into the atmosphere
Krakatoa	1883	The loudest explosion
Pelee Martinique	1902	30,000 people cremated in 6 seconds
Katmai, Alaska	1912	North America's deepest crater

And, finally, this book includes a digest of trivia about other eruptions including St. Helens, Yellowstone and the Bermuda Triangle. A convincing theory on Atlantis, what happened to the dinosaurs, a volcanic explanation of Bible stories such as the parting of the Red Sea, and others all created by the world's largest historic eruption at Santorin in 1500 B.C.

It also discusses Mt. Erebus, a volcano that erupts pure gold dust, and Pelee that sent a stone obelisk one hundred times the size of the Washington Monument up a slow elevator where it stood above the volcano 180 days and then slowly went back down into the crater. If this doesn't sound beyond the power of man, how about the woman whose panties were eaten off the wash line by an eruption (Katmai, 1500 miles away in Alaska) or a volcano that erupted hotel sized boulders on Sakurajima,

Japan? The book also tells the good that comes from volcanoes, including a chapter on Atoll Island Building by the late James Michener and little known facts such as volcanoes as the only source of new water and probably all water on earth.

In summary, the significance of this book is that it reads like an action novel, yet brings into focus the facts about the greatest environmental challenges we currently face. This book revives the ancient concepts of volcano religion in which it is more clear now that volcanoes, not man, giveth and taketh away.

CHAPTER I

WHEN THE EARTH EXPLODES: VOLCANOES AND THE ENVIRONMENT

I have been a life long environmentalist (my father was an early president of "Keep America Beautiful"). I have also been an amateur volcanologist and volcano writer for the last 40 years, starting in 1952 when I was stationed on the side of Mt. Vesuvius as a young NATO officer. I have long been disturbed by man taking credit (or blame) for most of the environmental horrors I know are due to volcanoes and volcanic eruptions.

For this reason I must first define the real or imagined global air pollution problems commonly attributed to man and then preface the words 'Volcanoes and' to each of them. That's what this first chapter is all about – Volcanoes **and** Greenhouse… Volcanoes **and** Acid Rain… Volcanoes **and** the Ozone Layer… Volcanoes **and** Global Warming… Once we have established the global significance of these enormous earth exploding eruptions, we can get on with the ghoulishly entertaining and always amazing volcanic events in the most violent eruptions of all time. All of which will bring into real doubt man's arrogant claims that he can control or have the slightest affect on the balance of nature.

Volcanoes and Pollution

Volcanoes are the cause of *global* air pollution, and we have the greatest amount of global air pollution in the years following a great eruption. This is for two basic reasons. First, only volcanoes have the explosive power to erupt their air pollutants into the stratosphere. Second, only volcanoes turn out these air pollutants in quantities that are able to interrupt nature's worldwide system of checks and balances that control global air quality.

If the air pollutants from the burning of fossil fuels were in a quantity significant to affect global air pollution, we would still have the problem of how the gases get up into the stratosphere. The answer is simple. It cannot happen. The proof lies in Mexico City, Los Angeles and Copsa Mica (Rumania), our three most air polluted cities. In these cities, the air pollution is local and at the surface trapped by mountains blocking the lateral disbursement, and the smog just sits there. Why?

Because the gases are heavier than air, they come back down to earth through gravity or they stay down because they originated from factories and automobiles in the city. They do not go up into the stratosphere without volcanoes to propel them against gravity. A good example of this is freon from refrigerators. Knock a hole in your refrigeration and the freon goes down and sits like a low cloud from the floor up to a height of six inches. It runs down the basement stairs but it does not escape to your attic. The mere fact that the air pollution hangs tough in L.A. is proof that the gases do not and can not rise high enough to affect global air pollution. If they could go straight up, they would, and Los Angeles would have little or no air pollution.

At the risk of repeating ourselves, automobile, factory and air conditioner gases do not and can not affect the ozone layer, global warming, etc. As convincing as the scare politicians and politicized scientists may give in "educating" us with the contrary, only volcanoes can shoot the gases that high. Therefore, it is this and not man burning fossil fuels, that has caused the scare of global catastrophe cited in our worldwide environmental media blitz. Even the data that graphs global carbon dioxide increase offered as proof of man's proliferation of CO_2 in Al Gore's book *Earth in the Balance* was gathered from the observatory on top of Mauna Loa, an active volcano in Hawaii. It does not drift over the observatory to be observed half way across the Pacific.

Air pollution from Los Angeles does not significantly effect Montana, Georgia and the rest of this country or this entire globe because it can not, unless, of course, a volcano chooses to erupt in the middle of the San Andreas fault. The fact is that all of the gases, principally carbon dioxide, chlorine and sulfur compounds, which cause the smog in Los Angeles, originate in Los Angeles and stay in Los Angeles. These gases certainly can not and do not escape 20 miles up to the stratosphere to cause us problems in global warming, acid rain and other global air pollution but instead slowly seep downward. These problems, when and if they really occur, come only from erupting volcanoes which are far more numerous (about 30 a year) than we realize. Volcanic eruptions such as "El Chichõn" (Mexico, 1981) and Mt. Pinatubo (Philippines 1991) sent enormous quantities of these gases into the atmosphere 20,000 feet up. The gases from just one of these volcanoes is 20 times the entire amount man causes with his fossil fuels in a year.

Since these man made gases that could create air pollution are "heavy," (more dense than air) the only way they can disperse is to move laterally from their source. In situations like Los Angeles and Mexico City, they cannot readily escape because mountains hold them in. When they can escape laterally, because of favorable winds, they still create little or no problem outside the immediate area as testified to by the people living in the L.A. suburbs over the mountains in Orange and San Bernardino Counties and the mountainside outskirts of Mexico City.

We can do something about our local air pollution and air quality. Sacrifice by limiting our lifestyle or by moving. Migration as civilizations always have done when their growing cities could no longer sustain their lifestyle as in Jericho, and the Maya cities of the Yucatan, to name a few. In these historic civilizations, changing climate made it impossible for the growing local urban area to sustain the lifestyle expected of an advanced culture.

The real danger to the world from man's somewhat arrogant thought that he can control all this is akin to Don Quixote. We simply cannot joust with volcanoes. We don't know what or how they erupt, much less how to stop them from erupting. When they erupt, we'd better be ready to move and move quickly (if temporary). Sooner or later they will erupt in great quantity as they have in the many past Ice Ages. But for now, their effects are being held in check by nature, which is the only force gigantic enough to do the job. At any rate, there is time. These things do not happen over night, and we should wait for testing to make sure that our billions of dollars have not been spent needlessly. It is not enough just to say there is global warming, for instance, because the majority of scientists may say so. We must sift the evidence, otherwise we'd still believe the earth was flat.

Al Gore in his very sincere book *Earth in the Balance* shows his political and journalistic background when he says, "Now we have developed the capacity to affect the environment on a global scale." He reflects his political conviction that man can do anything, but he can't, and we can't when it comes to controlling volcanoes and their singular effect on global air pollution.

We will go broke with the enormous cost of trying to control it, if indeed global air pollution is a universal problem, never mind the impossibility of man solving it. We would do much better to put away our trendy doomsday placards and march to the Serenity Prayer:

"God grant me the serenity to accept the things I cannot change, the courage to change the things that I can, and the wisdom to know the difference."

This book will show you that there is no immediate global warming trend and that if there was, it would be volcanoes and not man who might control it. Man has awakened to the discovery that the problems volcanoes create can be global. (Not all men, of course.) Volcanologists have known this for many centuries, but other scientists have only recently awakened to the volcanic impact on society.

Before we go into specific volcano eruptions and how they illustrate our fascinating story of life and death, let us review the current and somewhat trendy environmental terms and show how they relate almost entirely to volcanoes and most insignificantly to man's burning of fossil fuels and his leaky air conditioners. If you can, then accept this premise that volcanoes are the only significant cause, then we are on the way to a solution to our environmental trauma. At least we'll be able to separate the things we can and cannot do to help ourselves.

CHAPTER II

THE GAS THAT OFFENDS

*"Emissions control will not produce clean air
unless the EPA can figure out how to put a
filter on top of a volcano."*
– Buck Dawson

Every kind of gas you can imagine comes out when a volcano erupts, and in quantities so large that they dwarf man's excesses into insignificance.

The principal gas erupted from a volcano is H_2O, two parts Hydrogen and one part Oxygen (water as steam). In a *volcanic eruption*, H_2O exceeds all other gases combined by 7 to 1. This liquid (and its gas) is also the dominant substance on the earth's surface, and it occurs almost nowhere else in our universe. All of earth's new water comes from volcanoes, and according to University of Texas volcanologist Fred Bullard, "All water always has come from volcanoes." This molecular water vapor often combines with other gases to reach the earth as compounds such as sulfuric acid (acid rain).

How do volcanoes give us new water? Igneous rocks in the form of lava and granite contain 1% water. Assuming original magma contains 4% water, this would mean 3% is released during the crystallization process which occurs during igneous rock making. By this basis, William Rubey concluded in 1951 that the process involving a shell of igneous rocks 40 kilometers thick throughout the world would be sufficient to account for all the water in the oceans. The rock shell around the earth is much more than 40 kilometers thick.

Next come the carbon compounds that form mostly as *carbon dioxide*, also in gigantic quantities. Carbon dioxide is the #1 gas emitted from volcanoes excluding water vapor. The CO_2 from one eruption such as El Chichõn, Mexico in 1981 was in excess of 30 million metric tons and stayed in the atmosphere for three years, but this was small compared with Tambora in 1815 which hurled 100 times that amount into the stratosphere. It is CO_2 that is the principal gas in the controversial "Greenhouse Effect."

The third major gas from volcanoes is in the form of sulfur compounds such as *sulfur dioxide* which becomes sulfur trioxide and then sulfuric acid, as in acid rain. Sulfur dioxide stays high in the sky longer than most of the other volcanic chemicals and comes down as many as seven years after the eruption.

A fourth harmful gas that erupts in enormous quantities is *chlorine*, usually in the form of chlorine nitrate which is the chemical that causes "the hole" and which fights ozone in the Antarctic.

The gases coming from volcanoes vary widely from eruption to eruption, but the above four are always in quantity supply. They are natural gases far in excess of those given off by fossil fuels and CFC's or other surface air pollutants, the ratio is at least 20 to 1.

Fossil fuels, as in the burning of, provide 90% of man's source of energy. Formerly (until the 1930s and 40s) they consisted primarily of bituminous coal, a smoky sulfur laden source of local and surface air pollution. Our factories and trains burned this type of coal almost exclusively. Beginning in the 1940s, this source was gradually replaced with cleaner burning diesel oil and particularly natural gas. Man has also given up, at least in North America, the fertilizing practice of burning off his fields, burning leaves and heating homes with coal and wood.

Fuel for our automobiles may be a different matter, although our cars now get twice the miles per gallon and in all lead free gasoline. There are almost twice as many people in the U.S. (132, 164, 569 in the 1940 Census as opposed to 248, 709, 873 in the 1990 Census), and we are driving more cars but using cleaner burning engines. Our current way of life may cause an insignificant amount of pollution, but certainly not the problem it is purported to be on our global environment where termites produce almost twice as much carbon dioxide as man burning fossil fuels.

So that we completely understand, let's briefly go over the pollution terms that are being thrown at us by the press and politicians on predicting doomsday if we fail to clean up our act.

Greenhouse, Ice House or Out House

A lot has been voiced about the Greenhouse Effect as a cause of global warming. My volcano related premise is that the historic evidence points more to Ice House than Greenhouse, but Al Gore and his scientifically suspect evidence of global warming points more to Greenhouse and specifically Greenhouse gases caused by man. Here is a partial explanation of what it is and why it is or IS NOT significant to global warming.

The Greenhouse Effect is so called because CO_2 (carbon dioxide) and other "Greenhouse gases" are supposed to heat up the earth, acting as glass does in a greenhouse. These gases form a powerful heat trap and have been doing so according to the theory, since the Industrial Revolution began in the 19th Century, but particularly now with more people burning more fossil fuels to create more "greenhouse gases".

The question is one of maintaining a delicate balance, a balance nature probably strikes with little or no help from man. Without some Greenhouse Effect warming our planet, life would not be possible. The Greenhouse gases, primarily water vapor (including clouds), a large measure of carbon dioxide from many sources, such as volcanoes, the burning of fossil fuels, termites, oceans, animals breathing plus other gases such as methane and possibly man-made chloroflurocarbons warm our planet.

Most of this is on the surface of the earth and possibly in the lower atmosphere, and without this Greenhouse Effect, temperatures on earth would be below freezing. That is, the same CO_2 that could result in "burning us up" also keeps us from freezing.

Used in the current environmental sense, however, "Greenhouse Effect" means too much and not too little of the above gases perhaps causing 'global warming'.

Venus, for example, has 60,000 times more carbon dioxide in its atmosphere than earth, and its temperatures average above 800 degrees F., so we can see that "The Greenhouse Effect," if in fact there is such a thing going on in the world, could become a serious problem if the carbon dioxide balance gets out of hand. With too much CO_2 we could be in serious trouble. Most of this is in theory, not fact, unless we turn to volcanoes, the only significant source of CO_2 in the outer atmosphere. At any rate, carbon dioxide is turned out from many sources, several of which exceed man's most self indulgent figures for the burning of fossil fuels. For example, fossil fuels, termites, the oceans and our breathing combined are insignificant in comparison to volcanoes as the amount erupted from one volcano is in a ratio of 20 to 1, the one being all other sources combined, according to climatologist Iben Browning. *Greenhouse* is logical and real, but its effects on climate and global warming have yet to be proven.

What is El Niño?

If Greenhouse gases caused by man did not produce the heated summer in 1988 then what did? The answer to that question is a combination of normal but unpredictable weather cycles plus hundreds of erupting submarine volcanoes warming a large patch of the Pacific Ocean, called El Niño, which moved easterly with the wind and caused unpredictable weather all over the west coast.

El Niño is a weather phenomenon that comes to Ecuador and Peru about Christmas time, and therefore takes the Spanish name meaning Christ Child. El Niños are the curious warm patches (one at a time) that crop up in the Pacific Ocean about twice every ten years. These rather huge areas seem to affect the climate (weather) along the West Coast of North and South America and sometimes Africa. They last 12-18 months.

Some scientists speculate that the "El Niño" actually contributes to global warming, and that it helps offset the global cooling that occurs after a land based volcanic eruption throws vast quantities of carbon dioxide into the stratosphere, temporarily deflecting sunlight from the earth. Other scientists and writers, this author included, disagree on any true global affect. Within the California-sized or smaller El Niño patch, the Pacific is warmed up as much as four degrees Fahrenheit but only within the patch. There has never been an El Niño large enough to change the mean temperature of the vast Pacific Ocean even one degree.

Of interest from the perspective of this book is the part that submarine volcanoes play in El Niño. Recent undersea exploration mapping the Pacific sea bed discovered a record 1,133 "sea mound" volcanoes in an area about the size of California, 2,000 miles west of South America. Ken McDonald, the exploration team leader from the University of California (Santa Barbara) calls it "The greatest concentration of volcanoes so far to be found any where on earth, with some of the volcanoes so close together that they have erupted on top of each other, forming ocean bottom ridges up to 300 miles long."

Such a concentration of active volcanoes, many erupting at the same time, certainly may answer the mystery of what causes the El Niño, even though the resulting huge warm patch of water may drift quite a distance from the original eruptions. Add to that many volcanoes erupting H_2O directly into the ocean may also make it easier to understand how volcanoes cause the new water source on earth.

El Niño is an interesting phenomenon of the volcanic world that should be followed closely and studied for side effects since the warmest three years of the 1980s ('81, '83, '88) seem to follow El Niño events in the Pacific. These natural causes could be a factor in the real or imagined trend called global warming. These ocean warm spots are much more of a factor than man's burning fossil fuels and the Greenhouse Theory, although they hardly explain how they have caused record cold winters in the 1990s. Enough to say there is nothing new about El Niño in spite of the political and media blitz since we have become conscious of it. Every flood or weather crisis is now blamed on El Niño. It is the current trendy thing to blame.

The Ice House Effect

There is, of course, a paradox here in Greenhouse or Ice House, as there is in most complicated balances of nature. It is ironic that the same chemical compound that could create the Greenhouse Effect also creates an Ice House Effect in that the CO_2 is also responsible for deflecting the sunlight at higher altitudes, keeping the heat from reaching the earth in the same manner as it holds it in at lower altitudes. It works like the two sides of a blanket. Because of the Ice House Effect, there was a cold period, call it a mini Ice Age, although it lasted but a few years following the eruptions of Skaptor Jokel in Iceland (1783) and again after Tambora in Indonesia (1815). These eruptions, with their outpouring of CO_2-plus-dust deflecting the sunlight, caused years without summers and snow in July for two consecutive summers. Ben Franklin's account of the 1784 "summer" in Europe is particularly interesting. (Chapters to follow on these two great eruptions and find out about the world wide crop failure, the pestilence and even the political unrest they caused including the French Revolution.)

The big Ice Ages were undoubtedly originated by great volcanic activity causing dust clouds which circled the earth with CO_2 thousands of years ago. But let's not look too far in the past. Pinatubo (Philippines, 1991) and El Chichõn (Mexico, 1981) sent great emissions of carbon dioxide and other molecular dust particles into the stratosphere and caused North America's coldest winter in 74 years (1994-95 and 1995-96).

This deflection of sunlight to the earth, together with volcanic ash covering the leafy food supply, was the cause of the dinosaurs disappearance after dominating the earth's animal kingdom for a million years or more. With no food and an abruptly changing climate, they were starved or frozen to death. In other words, the dinosaur became an endangered species not because of man's stone ax but because of volcanoes and their Ice House Effect. Certainly what happened to the dinosaurs could happen to man at any time, but it probably will not happen soon. At any rate, it's something over which man, be he a politician or scientist, big spender or tight wad, optimist or pessimist has absolutely no control. If you don't believe this, think how long man has been trying unsuccessfully to control the weather.

In 1988 we had a very hot summer, and in 1994 and 1997 we had a very cold winters. Government scientists and politicians reacted to the former and wrongly used previous volcanic evidence to show that the Greenhouse Effect was warming things up. If we are going to accept this premature evidence, let's at least give the Ice House gang the same benefit of the doubt.

Better yet, let's accept the fact that there's no current "trend" either hot or cold. Everything is under a microscope these days by (1) scientists trying to make a discovery that will get the university government grants and (2) by the media looking for a sensational story and (3) by politicians looking for votes. They nearly always react before the evidence is conclusive. One or two hot or cold years is no trend and no real cause for panic. (see attached graphs)

SO MUCH FOR POLLUTION AND ACID RAIN
Stratospheric Loading by Volcanoes and Man
(note that man is less than 3% although increasing slightly)

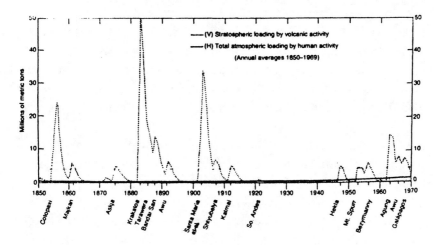

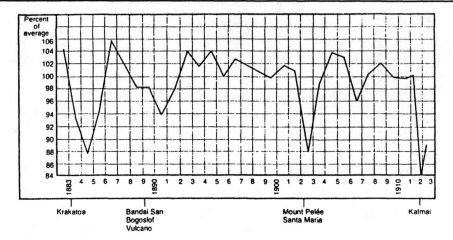

Krakatoa   Bandai San   Mount Pelée   Katmai
                Bogoslof   Santa Maria
                Vulcano

The Solar Radiation Graph indicates an alarming dip after a major eruption throws sun-deflecting dust into the Stratosphere

What is Acid Rain?

Chemically, acid rain is sulfuric acid, but it does not start out that way. Tremendous quantities of sulfur dioxide (over 20,000,000 tons from Pinatubo alone) are erupted into the stratosphere by volcanoes. Once shot off into the stratosphere, the sulfur dioxide from the volcanoes combines with oxygen at great altitudes to make sulfur trioxides, and eventually with vaporized H_2O (water) to make sulfuric acid.

A microscopic spray of these tiny droplets of sulfuric acid forms a fine mist and stays suspended in the atmosphere up to five years. The effect is world wide, and it peaks three years out when the sulfuric acid comes back to earth as acid rain. This differs from the volcano's primary effect, which is sun blocking dust that falls primarily in the first two years after the eruption.

The equator seems to be the inhibitor to rapid transmission of volcanic debris, including sulfuric acid. This phenomena has only recently been explained by ozone production from above the equator is the extreme heat and thin air (see the battle of ozone in this chapter). The debris from El Chichõn, Mexico, one of the dirtiest eruptions on record, took six months to diffuse to the North Pole, whereas debris from southern hemisphere volcanoes have a much more delayed effect taking as much as one year to diffuse across the equator. The northern hemisphere with El Chichõn, Mt. Pinatubo and St. Helens all on this side of the equator has had more than its share of acid rain since 1981.

Acid rain, taking two to seven years to come back to earth, may or may not be creating dead lakes in northern Ontario and blighting the Maple trees, but the source was definitely volcanoes in Mexico, the Philippines and the state of Washington which caused more than 100 times the normal acid rain output. The acid rain of the '80s and early '90s in Ontario was not caused by the much maligned smokestacks in Cleveland and Sudbury. If you don't believe this, then study the incidence of acid rain and see that it followed by months to several years, the eruptions of St. Helens (1980), El Chichõn (1981) and Mt. Pinatubo (1992).

The most dramatic close-to-every-home example of acid rain happened during North America's greatest historic eruption of Katmai in 1912 in Alaska. A housewife in Seattle, Washington was hanging her undies on the wash line in her back yard. She came out of her house a few hours later and found her panties in shreds, eaten by a volcano 1500 miles away. Egged on by a local radio station, the housewife wrote her soap company complaining.

Cutting Down the Rain Forest

The process of trees taking in CO_2 and giving off oxygen is called photosynthesis, and it is most effective with grass not trees. The carbon dioxide that some scientists say affects global warming is not increased by cutting down Rain forests. In fact, climatologist Iben Browning is quick to point out that Rain forests cut off sunlight reaching the ground and act as a breeding ground for termites, whose veracious appetites give off nearly twice as much CO_2 as all of man's burning of fossil fuels. If "eating" of CO_2 is the reason for not cutting down the rain forests, it is not a good one, for there is a lot more carbon dioxide consumed by a field of grass pastureland than there is by an equal size field of trees. The rain forests may be important for erosion control, preservation of water sheds and such industries as tourism and biotechnology, but certainly they are insignificant in prevention of global warming.

Two decades ago, the choice was simple "According to University of Pennsylvania biologist Daniel Janzen, 'Either the forest stood there or someone tore it down to plant a crop.' " This is also the way it happened 100 years ago all over Wisconsin, Pennsylvania, Michigan and Ontario, and it has grown back everywhere that the farms are not active. Fortunately the politicians in the tropical countries have already seen the light or maybe it is because pastureland and farms have already been established everywhere that deforestation is easy.

Research by Sandra Brown at Illinois and Boltkinan Simpson at the University of California (Santa Barbara) showed the carbon content of forests has been vastly over estimated. They suggest that deforestation is not the great source of CO_2 that we once thought. Rain forests are quite simply an insignificant factor in the Greenhouse and global warming concepts.

Madame Bovine's Moo Pooh

Now for the Outhouse Theory, as I think it's time in this grim session about man's folly in jousting with volcanoes for a little bathroom humor. "Madame Bovine" will certainly never rate with Flaubert's *Madame Bovery* as a literary masterpiece. As far as volcanoes are concerned, we can make the usual claim. All the cow poop in the world cannot equal the stench of rotten eggs (SO_2) coming from one volcano.

The cow poop theory of global warming is advocated by Jeremy Rifkin in his controversial book *Beyond Beef: The Rise and Fall of the Cattle Culture.* According to Rifkin, cattle ranching causes global warming by giving off methane gas. Most scientists disagree with Rifkin's sensational claims as he blames beefcakes for everything from the destruction of the tropical forests for building ranches, over grazing that destroys the grasslands and even world hunger because Madame Bovine eats too much grain. All this must be music to the ears of trendy vegetarians, but it does not make sense to anybody else. Ferdinand, for instance, thought he was smelling flowers all these years. If in fact Rifkin's theories were valid, the methane harm would have been most notable when the great herds of buffalo went poop poop pooping along our western plains or at least wherever the grass grew greenest.

It is ironic that in Rifkin's outrage over cutting the rain forest, destroying the Everglades, etc., he is championing two great swampy areas that produce far more methane gas than a bloated bellowing cattle herd ever could. And even these great swamps run a poor second to volcanoes. Not only do volcanoes erupt many times more methane gas than do cows, termites, swamps, garbage dumps and sewer plants combined, but underwater volcanoes and their methane gas are one of the few unanswered theories as to what may have caused the complete disappearance (with no visible trace) of aircraft in the Bermuda Triangle. (see chapter 8)

Suffice to say, the cattle waste theory is strictly bullshit and no serious scientist can take Rifkin seriously. Even Al Gore raises cattle as his non political business. Politicians in the great state of Texas, who have always been active in throwing a great deal of cow poop, have spent considerable time on a discussion on the importance of finding a cattle fodder that is less fart producing. I'm sure the taxpayers of Texas might add their endorsement to the politician proposing such a bill with the universal comment "May the wind at your back, Senator, always be your own!" Incidentally Texas and Tennessee rate 1st and 2nd as our biggest polluters of all states and provinces in the U.S. and Canada with Ontario 3rd in a 1997 report, "Taking Stock," issued by the United Nations for NAFTA.

Burning the Grasslands

As with animal grazing, and what comes after grazing, the pot ash from the age old controlled burning of the grasslands helps to green up the fields rather than destroy them. Grass fires usually are another of nature's (and man's) way of fertilizing the fields. These fires add nitrate to the soil and produce greener carbon dioxide eating grasses for everybody. Even the biggest fires, be they from the oil wells burning in Kuwait after Desert Storm or grass and forest fires burning out of control in central Africa, all are too small to add more than a fraction of one percent to the carbon dioxide emitted from a single volcano eruption.

The Orange County Register COLUMNS Sunday, Sept. 5, 1993
COMMENTARY 3

Too late, the holes in the ozone theory begin to widen

N ow that autumn is approaching and there's a hint of coolness in the air, it's time to recharge your automobile air conditioner. If you wait, you may find that the job — which two years ago cost perhaps $25 — will soon require a "retrofit" priced anywhere from $275 to $800. All car conditioners need infusions of the coolant known as CFC-12 every two or three years. Yet this substance, scheduled to be banned entirely by 1996, is already on its way out, and its substitutes will require expensive investments in new equipment.

The banning of CFCs has been mandated because they are deemed to deplete the ozone layer that shields us from cancer-causing ultraviolet (UV) radiation. Nor are these the only chemicals outlawed. In January, the Bush administration banned methyl bromide, a safe anti-fumigant and preservative, and halons, the best agents for extinguishing fires.

These prohibitions will cost consumers trillions while exposing countless people to greater risk from cancer and food poisoning. Yet they are unnecessary, a product of what future historians may call scientific fraud.

The ozone scare is a false alarm triggered by the argument, known as the Rowland-Molina hypothesis, that CFC molecules rise to the stratosphere, where the sun's rays release chlorine atoms that thin the ozone layer, threatening to increase UV radiation.

This theory was promoted by Vice President Al Gore and environmentalists, who, touting the "Antarctic ozone hole" as proof, persuaded Congress to outlaw all supposed ozone-depleting chemicals.

But many scientists long insisted there are many reasons to believe the Rowland-Molina hypothesis is wrong. They noted:

► Few CFCs reach the upper stratosphere, where they supposedly do damage.

► Volcanoes release nearly 30 times as much ozone-depleting chlorine as CFCs.

► The "ozone hole" was discovered by

the British researcher Gordon Dobson in 1956, long before CFCs were in general use.

► Ozone levels follow sunspot cycles and have risen, not declined, since the sunspot minimum in 1986-7.

► UV radiation is not increasing, and even the predicted rises are too small to pose much risk.

And last spring, more troubling evidence against Rowland-Molina surfaced. A study by Polish scientist Zbigniew Jaworowski reported that "the mass of chlorine from sea salt entering the stratosphere is about 500 times greater than the mass of CFCs, and this is just one of the terrestrial sources." Thus CFCs couldn't possibly cause a significant UV rise because they are infinitesimal compared with natural sources of ozone-depleting chemicals.

With a few exceptions, the press failed to report these doubts. Only this year, in

a so-called "ozone backlash," has the mainstream media begun to raise questions. Last spring, *The Washington Post* reported with apparent surprise that scientists cannot "find any solid evidence that serious harm was or is being done."

But the media's new-found skepticism comes too late to help you and me. Coolant prices are already rising faster than air balloons. Two years ago, the cost of CFC-12 was 50 cents per pound. Today, it is $10, and by 1996, it will be $25 — if you can find it. By that time, only around 15 percent of the needed supply will be available.

And since existing technology won't work with new coolants, simple recharging will require expensive retrofits. Retrofits will require $200 billion-$300 billion annually until the year 2000, and rebuilding "chillers" (big building air conditioners) will take billions more. But the old coolants will disappear before these conversions can be completed, leaving thousands of offices and re-

frigerator trains hot and humid.

Meanwhile, the substitutes pose new problems. Because many are highly caustic, air-conditioner life will be a fraction of what it is today. One, HFC 134a, has been found to cause tumors in rats. CFCs used in household insulation are being "supplanted by other substances whose dangers are not well understood. Some halon replacements are toxic. There are few safe substitutes for methyl bromide.

These are the costs of environmental hysteria. America has willfully invited soaring coolant prices, refrigeration shortages, air conditioning shut-downs, and increased public exposure to toxic chemicals and gastrointestinal disease.

The scare-mongers are right about one thing. Global warming will become reality. But this will happen indoors, not outdoors, when the air conditioning shuts off.

Mr. Chase is a syndicated columnist who writes about the environment.

Letters

Nobel Extrapolators?

This letter was sent to Chemical & Engineering News *in response to its Oct. 9, 1995, editorial attacking those who questioned the ozone depletion "consensus." It is printed here with permission of its author, Hugh W. Ellsaesser, Ph.D., who is a participating guest scientist at the Global Climate Research Division of Lawrence Livermore National Laboratory. Ellsaesser's article, "A Rational View on Stratospheric Ozone: The Unheard Arguments," appeared in the* Fall 1994 *issue of* 21st Century.

To the Editor [of *C&E News***]:**

In response to your editorial of Oct. 9, may I present a few facts about stratospheric ozone.

The original Rowland/Molina theory predicted the major destruction of ozone by chlorine would be at about 40 km. Observations show some decline there but generally less than that predicted; this is described as "broad agreement."

Formation of the Antarctic ozone hole, which occurs between 12 and 22 km, was not predicted.

Observations "show that much of the downward trend in ozone occurs below 25 km"; therefore, this also was not predicted.

Models including the chemistry involving sulfate aerosol and polar stratospheric clouds "still underestimate the ozone loss by factors ranging from 1.3 to 3."

As NASA's Dr. Robert Watson, organizer and director of the Ozone Trends Panel, told *Science,* "[our ozone] models do not predict that ozone decreased the way it did over the Northern Hemisphere during the past 17 years" (*Science,* Vol. 239, p. 1489, 1988).

As Harvard's Professor Jim Anderson told *The New York Times Magazine:* "The thinning of the ozone layer over other parts of the Earth is accelerating, and we don't know why, and we don't know how fast. We don't know what factors control the movement of ozone in the stratosphere. We don't know what part of the thinning is due to natural dynamics of the atmosphere and what part is due to the destruction of ozone by man-made chemicals. We don't know much of anything. . . . We've confused computer models of the atmosphere with the real thing. We're making huge extrapolations based on nothing but models, and models are often wrong" (*The New York Times Magazine,* March 13, 1994, **pp.** 36-39).

I have a question. On what criterion was the Nobel Prize awarded to Crutzen, Molina, and Rowland?

(All quotes without attribution are from the Executive Summary of the World Meteorological Organization's *Scientific Assessment of Ozone Depletion, 1994.*)

Hugh W. Ellsaesser
Livermore, California

What is Ozone?

Ozone is pure oxygen, and it is all good. It fights pollution, and it is not part of it. Ozone (O_3) is a globe circling protective layer of gas that shields the earth from the sun's cancer causing UV (ultraviolet) radiation. When it absorbs this radiation, it breaks down into "nacent" atomic (O) oxygen and molecular (O_2) oxygen.

Atomic Oxygen (O) forms when molecular (O_2) oxygen rises to the upper atmosphere. When (O) and (O_2) are exposed to direct sunlight near the outer reach of the atmosphere, they re-combine to form (O_3) or ozone. This only occurs near the equator where the sun's direct rays are the hottest and most constant. No ozone is created at the poles because the tilt and rotation of the globe shields the poles from the hot and direct sunlight even during the summer months.

Hence, ozone, which is created naturally only in the stratosphere above the equator, was observed by astronauts in the space shuttle, racing in streams moving toward the South Pole to fill in the depleted ozone layer over the south polar ice cap.

What is Not Ozone

"Low Level Ozone." This commonly used term for the smog often created in summer humidity over natural forests and in man made cities is a great misnomer. It is certainly confusing to the public. It is not ozone by any means. Ozone is made of pure oxygen treated to intense equatorial sunlight at very high altitudes. "Low level ozone" is part of "smog," a mixture of many other very disagreeable elements, one of which is oxygen. The public understands smog. It is confusing and alarming and perhaps out right lying for the EPA to advertise smog as "Low level ozone."

Hole in the Ozone

In 1956, 40 plus years ago, an "ozone hole" was discovered near the South Pole by Gordon Dobson, a British scientist. Dobson nor any other scientists know how many years, centuries or millenniums the "hole in the ozone" has been there. The "hole" exists only near the South Pole and only during certain seasons. This is the one and the only hole in the ozone. Only at the South Pole is the combination of intense cold that can create a hole in the ozone.

The hole in the ozone doubled in two years during and immediately after Pinatubo (1991-1993) and then shrank again to its original pre-eruption size in less than two more years. Yet, during this period of hole expansion, the environmental alarmists, through our politicians, initiated a huge spending hole in our deficit to restrict the use of CFC-12 and other supposedly ozone depleting chemicals.

Maybe volcanoes can help us make up our minds. Pinatubo certainly went a long way toward disproving half baked scientific theories. To say that CFCs are dangerous environmentally is fraudulent and irresponsible guesswork. CFC depletion of the ozone has never been measured, and since they have already been banned, they will never be measured. Atomic testing, chemical fertilizers and the supersonic jet are other things that were banned because they might deplete the ozone long before we had "invented" CFCs, but none of these things will wreck the havoc that we will suffer in our "comfort zone" and our economy when CFC's are no longer produced. We may pay up to 25 times the total amount for air conditioning, for use of much less efficient refrigeration chemicals, only to find that some other politicized scientists guess that they, too, might affect our atmosphere.

Somehow we must seize control of our economy and our "clean" air from these so called scientists before we go broke. It seems a know-no for scientists to speak up and chance fouling up their universities getting government environmental grants unless the results verify the party line. We deemed this sort of politicized science as beyond the pal when it was practiced by Joseph Goebels and the Third Reicht in the period before and during WWII, yet today it is accepted "scientific" practice to jump to conclusions based on incomplete data when the conclusion backs up a hurried act of Congress or a premature finding of the EPA. All of which leaves us with volcanoes we can do nothing about unless it's to go bankrupt trying to control a situation we cannot control.

"The public has been misled, bamboozled, and otherwise manipulated," Dr. S. Fred Singer told Congress. Here, he chats with Rep. Rohrabacher (center) and Rogelio Maduro (left), author of the book The Holes in the Ozone Scare.

HOUSE HEARINGS CHALLENGE SCIENCE MAFIA ON OZONE, CLIMATE

Congressional hearings on ozone depletion and on climate models, sponsored by the House Committee on Science's subcommittee on energy and environment, held Sept. 20 and Nov. 16, made it clear that the ban on chlorofluorocarbons (CFCs) is determined by politics, not science; that climate models known to be faulty were used to determine international policy; and that the science establishment is willing to act like a gestapo to prevent scientific dissent on environmental policy.

Subcommittee chairman Dana Rohrabacher (R-Calif.) convened both hearings under the title "Scientific Integrity and Public Trust: The Science Behind Federal Policies and Mandates" and invited both sides of the issues to testify. The ozone hearings were particularly vituperative. The airing of the main scientific arguments against the ozone hoax provoked some congressmen and administration spokesmen to attack those scientists who disagreed with the "consensus" view as "fringe," "irresponsible," and "without standing in the scientific community."

Dr. S. Fred Singer, head of the Science and Environmental Policy Project and an emeritus professor of environmental science at the University of Virginia, and Dr. Sallie Baliunas, an astrophysicist, came under particular fire. Baliunas testified that she had almost pulled out of participating in the hearing that morning because of the ongoing threats to her and her employer. She also told the committee that she was warned not to pursue lines of research that might show the ozone depletion theory to be wrong, because her institution might lose federal and other funding.

Baliunas's testimony is available from the Marshall Institute (202) 296-9655; Singer's testimony is available from SEPP (703) 934-6940.

Hearings in November on the validity of the global climate models were less stormy, but the same arguments were used to maintain that the global warming scenario is correct simply because, allegedly, "the overwhelming majority of scientists" agree that it is.

GERMAN SPECTROMETER PRODUCES GLOBAL OZONE MAP IN 3-D

A new German spectrometer called Crista, deployed on the U.S. Space Shuttle in 1994, has produced the first high precision, 3-dimensional global map of ozone, announced researchers from the University of Wuppertal, who designed the instrument. The ozone layer is a patchwork of large- and small-scale structures and not a uniform longitudinal phenomenon, the researchers said. Crista's preliminary results show that the currently accepted ozone models are "junk," they said at a Nov. 6 press conference. More details will appear in the next *21st Century*.

❚ TALK SHOW

The big ozone lie is still being repeated

There are two ways to tell a lie ["Dannemeyer's wrong about ozone problem," Letters, Oct. 24]. The first is to just state something completely false. The second is more devious, like the used-car salesman who tells you the engine is good, the brakes are good, but doesn't tell you about the transmission that's about to blow. He has lied by omission.

CFCs' capability to destroy ozone is true. What Stanley Tyler and Ralph Cicerone "forgot" to mention is that more than 99 percent of the destruction is caused by natural forces; namely the eruption of volcanos that spew millions of cubic yards of chlorine and fluorine (natural gases) into the ozone layer, which is at about 83,000 feet.

Twenty years ago, the bulk of the text of speeches against CFCs was in regard to slowing American development of computer circuit boards so the Soviet Union could advance its own computer industry in the world market. CFCs are indispensable to the making of circuit boards.

Today, the argument against CFCs is either by those on the far left or researchers playing the "government grant game." Get to the media. Scare the public. Get a million dollars.

And to answer critical readers, I have earned three college degrees, one of them for meteorology.

James Todhunter
Newport Beach

SCIENCE WATCH/LEE DYE
Flouting the Ozone Doomsayers

It is not a matter of how many scientists agree with such logic – it was once thought the world was flat. Sallie Baliunas of the Harvard-Smithsonian Center for Astrophysics feels like a very small fish swimming up a very swift stream. She is one of the world's leading experts on the physics of the sun and she's now laying her impeccable scientific credentials on the line by taking a highly unpopular stand on a widely publicized question. The issue involves the ozone layer in the Earth's stratosphere, which protects life on this planet from the sun's cancer causing ultraviolet radiation. Research has shown that chlorofluorocarbons (CFCs) - notably the freon that is used to cool our buildings and refrigerate our food – destroys ozone.

Concern over the issue has been so intense that a 1987 treaty, the Montreal Protocol, will phase out the use of CFCs over the next few years - at a cost expected to run into the billions. Environmental leaders and many scientists have hailed the ban as proof that policy makers can be forced to make the right decisions, if the threat is great enough.

But debate over the need for the ban continues to rage. The most extreme opponents see the ozone threat as a myth generated by big government and greedy scientists, while others fervently insist any destruction of ozone will doom life on this planet. Passions are intense on both sides.

So why would a scientist like Baliunas inject herself into the fray and take a position of vehement opposition to the ban, even to the point of telling the Arizona Legislature that its residents will be in no physical danger if the state refuses to abide by the ban?

She believes the ban resulted from blatant corruption of science, and that troubles her far more than the perceived threat of ozone depletion.

"I've been told by some people that what I am doing is evil," she said, "because it's a danger to humanity, yet when I look at the data I'm hard pressed to see exactly what the danger is."

Her greatest concern, she said, is "working in a system that's corrupt, that won't look at all the facts."

Baliunas concedes that synthetic chemicals are depleting the ozone, as the National Aeronautics and Space Administration claimed last December it had proved. But she insists that the impact is minor compared to natural fluctuations in the ozone layer.

And there is plenty of time to collect and weigh the evidence before ozone depletion becomes a public health hazard, if indeed it ever does.

There is not enough space here – nor is there enough evidence anywhere – to resolve this debate. But Baliunas' searing indictment of her fellow scientists should make anyone step up and take note.

I've been told by scientists that it doesn't matter what the facts say because we are getting policy makers to do the right thing," she said. That infuriates her, enough to take what she characterizes as a "big professional risk" that could result in ostracism from the scientific establishment.

Baliunas' main criticisms:

• There is no significant effort to measure the level of ultraviolet radiation reaching the ground, and the few scattered attempts to do so have shown mysteriously that the radiation has decreased, not increased, when global levels of ozone have been depleted. "You would like to know exactly the level of ultraviolet coming in," she says, and it is easy to measure it "There's no reason to guess. Just measure it."

• The ozone layer is affected by many natural events, including volcanoes and seasonal weather patterns, that dwarf the effect of synthetic chemicals. "There's a hundredfold difference in just seasonal swings compared to what the man-made depletion is." The increased risk from ultraviolet radiation caused by synthetic chemicals over the next decade would be about the same for someone in Southern California as moving 20 miles closer to the Equator, she said.

• The only place where synthetic chemicals seem to be having a real effect is over Antarctica, and then only during October. "It's very hard to find any major catastrophe pending there. Not many people live there," she said. Even NASA's research suggests that the problem is isolated over the South Pole. Extremely cold temperatures seem to be critical, which is why significant ozone depletion from manufactured chemicals has not been found anywhere else, even over the Arctic, NASA scientists concede.

Baliunas said the debate over ozone depletion is being driven by the "uncertainty principle." The principle holds that we must not allow the use of any chemicals or human processes "unless we are certain it causes no harm."

And such a principle is an offense to her professional ethics. "It happens to be an anti-scientific statement because in science you can never absolutely prove something. You can only get less and less uncertain."

There are many reputable scientists in the world who strongly disagree with Baliunas, and time may prove her wrong. But time, she says, is something we have plenty of. Instead of striving for a better understanding of the problem, she argues, we were stampeded into adopting a Draconian measure without knowing the real impact on public health.

Scientists who agree with her, she says, are reluctant to speak out because they don't want to discourage policy makers from making tough decisions when the evidence says they should. "But the evidence is unclear here", she contends. "The uncertainty principle is in full bloom."

We may have erred on the safe side, but Baliunas insists it was bad science. And in her view that trade-off is not worthwhile.

THE TORONTO STAR

Toronto Stocks at all-time high BUSINESS SECTION

DINO-MITE WHAT'S ON SECTION

Learning to live with the

THURSDAY, August 26, 1993

Chemical cutbacks put ozone layer on' mend

By Michael Smith
TORONTO STAR

The battered ozone layer could start recovering by the end of the decade because emissions of the two main chemicals that destroy it are slowing more quickly than expected, a U.S. researcher suspected.

But don't put away the suntan yet: It will take at least another century for the ozone layer to recover completely, according to James Elkins of the U.S. National Oceanic and Atmospheric Administration.

Elkins and colleagues studied emissions of two ozone-killing chemicals — the chlorofluorocarbons CFC-11 and CFC-12, which are used in refrigeration and air conditioning and to produce plastic foams.

They found that the growth in CFC-11 emissions has slowed to about 1 per cent a year, down from a peak of between 4 and 5 per cent in the 1980s. The growth in CFC-12 emissions is down to 2 per cent a year, from that same high level.

The research appears in today's edition of *Nature*, the British scientific journal.

"The good news is that we don't have this enormous growth rate," Elkins said. "The bad news is that these molecules have lifetimes of 50 to 100 years — they hang around for quite a long time.

"We expect to see the ozone layer start to improve at the beginning of the next century," he said.

But because of the longevity of the chemicals involved, it will take at least another 100 years for the ozone layer to return to normal.

Jim Kerr, head of ozone monitoring for Canada's Atmospheric Environment Service, said he wasn't surprised by the results: "We know production of CFCs has been dropping," he said.

But he added it will still be several years before the amount of CFCs in the atmosphere starts to drop: "It's going to be 10 years or so before we're on the downward slope," he said.

The good news comes as satellite data show that the ozone levels above many parts of the Earth's surface are at the lowest they've ever been.

Kerr said ozone levels over Toronto "have been continually below normal since the beginning of the year."

Elkins said this year's low ozone levels are also the result of "a curve ball thrown by nature" — the 1991 eruption of Mount Pinatubo in the Philippines. Such an eruption, he said, can severely reduce ozone levels for a short time, but the atmosphere bounces back within a few years.

The way our politicians and government controlled scientists cover their errors through an eager press is indicated by this front page story in the *Toronto Star*. It infers that man and not nature has somehow reduced the danger to the ozone when it was the volcano Pinatubo all along.

Is There a Global Warming Trend?

One of the real tests of our past global warming trends, if any, is with tree rings: depicting growth, short or long growing seasons, hotter summers, colder winters, etc. Most indicative are the growth rings from a 3,613 year old South American tree which show no signs of the climate being warmed due to human activity, according to Ricardo Villalba, a researcher from the University of Colorado and his research partner Antonio Lara from the University of Arizona. The tree rings checked are from alerce trees, the second longest living tree species known. Villalba measured the width of tree rings in 96 trunk wedges from standing alerce trees and from stumps of harvested trees in Chile and Argentina. The trees ranged in age from 325 to 2,248 years, and the grand daddy of them all was the 3,613 year old alerce tree.

This information was gleaned from a report in *Science Journal* for May, 1993 by Villalba and his team. The researchers were careful to point out that their studies did not contradict studies that may have showed warming trends in the northern hemisphere, but that their studies did indicate that any so called global warming isn't really global. The two scientists explained that by relating the tree ring growth with known temperatures recorded in the area over the past 100 years. The data was definitely verified so that the accuracy of the tree ring material could be established even in the years before temperature readings were available. Villalba said he and his co-worker could definitely establish a climate record that showed much higher temperatures <u>before</u> the beginning of the Industrial Revolution (a 500 year old oak tree in Connecticut revealed similar findings of no global warming).

Also of interest to those scientists attributing global warming to volcanoes and not to man burning fossil fuels is the additional data obtained by Villalba and his group that there were summer time temperature increases in South America from 1400 to 750 B.C. and from 80 B.C. to 160 A.D., both followed by long normal periods. The most recent warm "trends" were a 30 year period from 1729 to 1756 and another from 1800 to 1830. (There were also intervals of cooler climates noted from 770 to 570 B.C. and from 300 to 470 A.D. and from 1490 to 1700). The significant thrust of Villalba's data is that it showed wide swings in average temperatures over the last 3000 years but "We can say there was NO indication of global warming ever caused by man at least in the area (tested)" according to Villalba.

We don't use tree rings alone to disprove the hypothesis of global warming. In and above the Arctic Ocean, 27,000 temperature readings have been taken over the past 40 years, and they show absolutely no warming trend. According to Jonathan Kahl, whose study is reported in *Nature*, these cold facts do not agree with the articulate James Hansen's computer models on the effects of adding carbon dioxide and lesser quantities of other gases to the atmosphere and forecasting a general warming trend. Kahl conceded his findings "Do not disprove the warming theory everywhere in the world, but if they (the computer models) are not getting the Arctic quite right, then maybe they are not getting the whole picture quite right."

It is ironic that not only is there no major regional warming in the Arctic, but none in Antarctica, above which is the hole in the ozone. This may be due to the heat from Antarctic undersea volcanoes, perhaps our biggest single factor in preventing a major melting in Antarctica.

These volcanoes, in almost continuous eruption, produce warmth that melts just enough ice to produce a layer of mud, over which ice (glaciers) migrating toward the sea move about one-half a mile a year (a rapid pace as such things move) for hundreds of miles to the seashore, in 30 to 60 mile wide ice rivers. They then move on out into the southern ocean to produce the "Ross Ice Shelf", a huge off shore shelf of ice, acting as a barrier, separating the comparatively warm ocean from the central ice reservoir. The Ross Ice Shelf actually shields and protects the main ice reservoir from ocean melting which really could cause world wide flooding if the warmer ocean currents had direct contact with the interior ice.

Many scientists and several scientific think tank conferences held both before and after the eruption of the volcano Pinatubo, have asked us to wait for more evidence before action is taken in the red badge of self blame for air pollution, at least as far as global warming is concerned. So much of the prevailing scare tactics of environmentalists and politicians have come from James Hansen's claims and his quotable computer model results, most of which have since been dismissed as premature or invalid. I would go farther and say up until this time we have no hard evidence of a global warming trend for the last several centuries.

As Richard Linzen, the eminent MIT environmental scientist points out, "Environmental legislation tends to be irreversible. It is not responsible to base conclusions on what sometimes appears to be scientific gibberish." Linzen deplores the most unscientific approach to environmental issues "where a mere call for action has become a litmus test for morality."

It seems to this author that whereas the Food and Drug Administration must prove its contentions before a product is taken off the shelves, the Environmental Protection Agency can ban a substance or regulate most anything on the flimsiest of evidence that it might be bad for society. "Scientists" who depend on government grants are pushed to substantiate what the politicians have already acted on, such as the U.S. Senate's unanimous vote on banning CFC's in a vote taken just before the 1992 election. While it may be true that most of us no longer have faith in politicians, we do believe in the integrity of scientists and scientific methods and yet "today, for the first time in democracies, we are seeing a politically-driven activity that superficially resembles science but scorns its underlying methods," according to Tom Bethell in *American Spectator*. Bethell goes on to say that "Environmentalists have figured out that science can be highjacked for ideological purposes." I am old enough to remember our outrage when the third Reich and Joseph Goebels treated science in such a way.

I am not questioning Vice President Gore's motives. His sincerity seems apparent and his research is thorough as far as it goes. In his book *Earth in the Balance: Ecology and the Human Spirit*, he owns up to a feeling for his family business (which is politics), his eight years of journalism and his ambitions to be President, all of which must lend themselves to some of his conclusions. Historically, he uses the same volcanic facts I use as examples of extreme climate and the economic conditions which followed the great eruptions of Skaptor Jokel (1783), Tambora (1815) and Krakatoa (1883).

He uses these most horrendous historic eruptions to illustrate what could happen today if man keeps indulging the excesses of his way of life. Gore's conclusions that man's excesses are causing a far worse situation is contrary to most emerging evidence and responsible scientific opinion however.

Al Gore says "Now that we have developed the capacity to affect the environment on a global scale, can we also be mature enough to care for the earth as a whole?" You would expect a politician to truly believe he or we could affect environment on a "global scale", but in fact it is arrogant to believe he or we can do anything. His continued plea is that we cannot leave our children and grandchildren with this so called environmental problem of "global warming".

I should not and would not guess at the Senate's mood before they collectively cast an unanimous vote to ban all CFC's except to say that their pre-election conclusion (1992) is dead wrong in blaming man, his fossil fuels and air conditioners for all these global environmental problems. All the arrogance, the government funded research grants that seem to be affecting the integrity of our major universities and the big spending from our near empty treasuries (promised at the Earth Conference by George Bush ($45 billion and another $4 billion from Canada's Prime Minister Mulroney)) will not help. There is no way we can spend enough or sacrifice enough to do battle with volcanoes. Volcanoes have a mind of their own. It is ridiculous that man should work himself into a panic, and that unscrupulous or poorly informed politicians should line up behind these issues to win over a frightened public. Someone is taking at best incomplete evidence and using it incorrectly. There is no hurry about any of this. It will take years for a real global warming trend to be evident. So let us take our finger off the panic button and sort out any real evidence.

Until science has been able to answer a lot more questions about global warming and a lot better way to feed data into its computer models, we'd better keep studying and avoid what looks more and more like the environmental extremists manipulating the public.

In case you still can't believe that all these governmental scientists, politicians, school teachers and newspapermen could be wrong about the environment, and you can't believe that volcanoes and not man are the culprits, read the chapters about what individual eruptions have done to our global, regional and local environment. It is a fascinating war and peace paradox.

Is the Earth Really Getting Warmer?

The graph below shows how much temperatures were predicted to rise, based on a highly regarded global warming computer model, versus the temperature changes actually measured by NASA satellites. The computer forecast, averaged over the past 15 years was more than three times the actual rise.

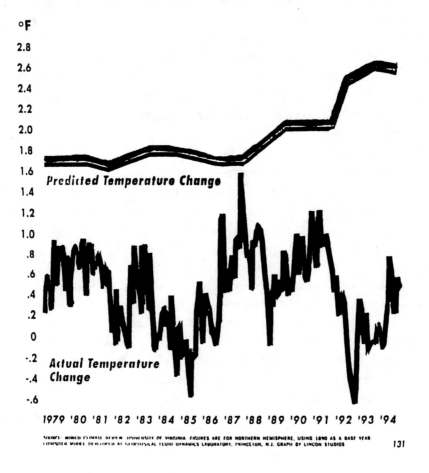

Source: World Climate Review, University of Virginia, figures are for northern hemisphere, using 1890 as a base year. Computer model developed at geophysical fluid dynamics laboratory, Princeton, N.J. Graph by Lincon Studios.

Temperatures are rising 0.1 degree Celsius a decade, three times less than computer projections, says a study that indicates global warming concerns are greatly exaggerated. "A growing body of evidence shows global warming is not a serious threat," says Sallie Baliunas, a Harvard astrophysicist who did the study for the George C. Marshall

Institute. Based on other studies, industrialized countries are being urged to cut carbon dioxide emissions, which are blamed for atmospheric heating.

Since none of the mini Ice Ages global melting or other worldwide climate changes have taken place since man's industrial revolution began 200 years ago, we are left with natural causes as the only *significant* cause – change in global climate.

These significant climate changes certainly occurred in our geological but not during man's written history. The seven most significant volcano eruptions during man's history, the last two right here in North America are detailed here. The remainder of this book gives us the fascinating story of the chaos and catastrophe that follows great eruptions. None of our earth day science fiction approaches the truth that these volcanoes have erupted our society.

CHAPTER III

THE VOLCANO THAT SET WESTERN CIVILIZATION BACK 1200 YEARS

THERA - NOW SANTORIN (1500 B.C.) IS WHY WE CAN'T FIND ATLANTIS

"Civilization exists by geological consent subject to change without malice."

- Will Durant

The children of Israel owe their survival to the volcano Thera, even as Atlantis owes its demise to the same volcano. It all occurred about 1500 B.C. when the volcano Santorin (Thera) erupted in the eastern Mediterranean with the most cataclysmic force yet known and since known to man. Its influence on the Bible stories of the Old Testament and its influence on Plato's Atlantis disappearing is both logical and about right in the time frame. To put it bluntly, this volcano started it all as far as we humans know the western world.

While many explorers have claimed discovery of "the lost continent of Atlantis" many places in the Atlantic Ocean just west of Africa and even in the Caribbean, they fail to consider Plato's point of reference. He knew nothing about the Caribbean and little about the Atlantic Ocean. It was an island, a large volcanic island which, as Plato said, disappeared "beneath the water in a day and a night." Says Dr. Robert Logan, "The volcano at Thera (Santorin) in the Aegean Sea erupted in 1500 B.C. and packed the power of 25,000 one mega-ton nuclear devices. This eruption ejected more than 65 to 100 cubic miles of earth. (Almost twice the quantity of airborne dust erupted by Tambora, the greatest air polluter of more modern history in 1815). It caused tidal waves 200 feet high that completely wiped out the Minoan civilization on nearby Crete which was nonetheless 90 miles away. Scholars now believe that Plato was referring to Thera in the *Republic* when he mentions the mysterious disappearance of an advanced culture, Atlantis, into the sea."

Plato lived from 427 to 347 B.C. He credits his story of Atlantis to Critias, an Athenian politician who heard it at 10 from his 90 year old grandfather who heard it from his father, a friend of Solon (a liberal who had been exiled to Egypt about 590 B.C.) who heard the story from priests in Egypt who had passed the story down from generation to generation. So 200 years later, after Critias' grandfather passed on the story, Plato wrote it all down.

Atlantis "the lost continent" as identified by Plato was not just the large island of Crete but all the other Cyclades as well. These now romantic Greek Islands are the tops of volcanoes, mountains on a large sunken land mass that stretches across the Aegean Sea from Greece to Asia Minor. The sum total of these islands with Crete were the home base of the Minoan civilization, each with individual identifying characteristics: mines, ship building and agriculture of the Minoan Bronze Age civilization. All these islands were, like the large island of Crete, swept clean by tidal waves and buried under the ash when Thera blew out of the island of Santorin in the middle of the Cyclades. Plato must have been referring to the long sunken land mass as the continent of Atlantis and the people of Crete and the mountain top volcanoes as the civilization wiped out in a day and a night by the greatest eruption yet known to man.

So much for Atlantis, it's not there anymore, but it's no longer the mystery that Plato once thought it was.

How One Volcano Wiped Out 3000 Years of Western Civilization

The importance of this great eruption in the eastern Mediterranean goes far beyond solving the riddle Plato poses in the disappearance of Atlantis. It shows how volcanic eruption wiped out our western culture which had been developing in the Bronze Age Minoan civilization for 3000 years and made us begin all over again in Ancient Greece.

The volcano Thera, in one enormous eruption, buried our roots for 3500 years, until archeologists dug out evidence in the last 50 years of the advanced civilization wiped out at its very zenith by a volcano. A civilization already 3000 years old gone as Plato said, "in a day and a night." Here is how it went as told through Plato's Atlantis, through the Bible stories of the Old Testament and through the archaeology just now being put together through the remnants of the 6500 year old Minoan civilization from mine shafts first excavated to mine the volcanic ash of so long ago to make the cement for modern Athens.

So who were these remarkable Minoans who dominated the Bronze Age for 3000 years only to be snuffed out in "a day and a night" forcing Western Civilization to start all over again on the mainland of Ancient Greece?

What remains of Atlantis alias Santorin alias Thera.

So Who Were These Minoans Anyway?

The Minoans, kings of the world during the Bronze Age, came by their throne by inventing the keel and using their keeled vessels to hop from island to island, ridding the seas of piracy and controlling commerce with their wisdom and military might. They were still gaining luster after 3000 years of dominance. Their pottery, metals, wheat and other grains, were the best in the Mediterranean world which was the root of the

European and eventually the western world culture we are a part of today. All of this was just beginning when this master race disappeared from the face of the earth.

They operated from a big island base on Crete and the many smaller islands, volcano tips known as the Cyclades in the Aegean Sea between the eastern Mediterranean between Greece, Turkey and Asia Minor where their ships controlled the then civilized world from the island of Rhodes on the east to Gibraltar on the west with their commerce going on land over much of southern Europe.

It seemed that there was nothing to stop them. They were a civilization in control, at its best, then suddenly they went from zenith to zip. They seemed to disappear from the face of the earth, their influence, their accomplishment, their very existence remained at best a subject of scientific debate until 3500 years later when Greek geologists, anthropologists and archaeologists accidentally discovered traces in a deep well on Crete and then dug in to discover more. Like Vesuvius' burying Pompeii and Herculaneum sealing them like a mud wasp in a tomb of volcanic mud and ash, the ruins on Crete and Santorin have begun to emerge as scientists piece together a 6500 year old mystery and gap in man's history destroyed but entombed for future study by volcanoes.

Such theories gleaned from Dr. Bullard's book, *Volcanoes of the Earth*, are a symposium of evidence by volcanologists, seismologists and archeologists only recently brought to this conclusion by the excavations of George Galanopoulos of the University of Athens. It was Galanopoulos who came upon the ruins of a stone house and found wood and human teeth dating to 1500 B.C., all at the bottom of a mine shaft on Thera, dug to mine volcanic ash for the cement plants in Athens.

The ash from the remains of Atlantis is now the paving cement that holds together the building blocks of the current Greek civilization. Volcanoes have a way of preserving the history of civilization sealed in the mudslides of Herculaneum below Vesuvius and buried in the ash from Santorin even though they originally destroyed the life that was. As to "Atlantis" we can stop looking. It simply is not there any more because it was blown to smitherines.

Profile showing San Torini before and after

Santorin (Thera) erupted about 1500 B.C. The eruption was so great that it was estimated to be nearly twice the size and power of Tambora (1815). The whole top of the mountain must have fallen into the molten mass below the caldera and come back with an explosion that sent tidal waves and total darkness all over the Eastern Mediterranean.

There was once an island, Thera, in the Eastern Mediterranean with a dormant volcano on its highest point. The Minoan civilization there was the most advanced in the Bronze Age. Suddenly the civilization disappeared never to be seen of heard again. Much later, Plato wrote about the disappearance of Atlantis; this all happened about 1600 years before Christ.

Volcanoes Provide Scientific Basis for Many Old Testament Stories

> *He looketh on the earth and it trembles*
> *He toucheth the mountains and they smoke.*
>   Psalms 104:32

> *"Then the Lord rained... fire and brimstone... and, lo, the smoke*
> *of the country went up as the smoke of a furnace."*
>   – Genesis 19:24-28

As a young boy it used to disturb me when my Sunday school teacher Mr. Ramsey read us the Bible but told us we were not to take the words literally but to interpret them in some modern way that I didn't understand any more than Moses turning over his hand to get darkness and the parting of the Red Sea to help children run away. I dismissed this explanation of what I saw in the good book until I began to study volcanoes. It was then that I found all these stories were based on what could and probably did happen when the volcano Thera erupted about the same time in history

Atlantis is not the only victim of Santorin. The Egyptian Army was also a victim as the Red (Reed) Sea parted to allow the children of Israel to escape and then roared back in a tidal wave of destruction, as seaside volcanoes are prone to do during great eruptions as evidenced much later in Mt. Pelee, Martinique, Krakatoa and Mono Loa.

Santorin provides a scientific explanation for the parting of the Red Sea and for Moses' three days of darkness. Biblical scholars set the date around 1500 B.C. and the "plague of darkness"... "And the Lord said unto Moses, stretch out thy hand toward heaven, that there may be darkness over the land of Egypt, even darkness which may be felt. And Moses stretched forth his hand towards heaven; and there was a thick darkness in all the land of Egypt for three days." An eruption the size and type of Thera would send enough ash (at least 65 cubic miles) into the sky to make the air as thick as it would be dark. We know in modern times that Krakatoa (1883) exploded to cause total darkness 120 miles distant for more than 22 hours. There were days of similar darkness in many of Vesuvius' eruptions. Katmai (Alaska) is the greatest North American eruption. It left Kodiak Island, 100 miles distant, in total darkness so impenetrable into the third day, that a lighted lantern could not be seen at arm's length, and Tambora (1815) left parts of Java, 300 miles distant, in total darkness for three full days. If Tambora why not Thera (Santorin), an even greater eruption with a similar collapsing caldera that took place centuries before?

Krakatoa in 1883, more than a century ago, presented us with another phenomenon with Biblical overtones if judged by a similar condition at the ancient Santorin. The eruption of Krakatoa caused waves 20 meters high in Java and Sumatra, 100 miles away.

The eminent seismologist Professor George Galanopoulus theorizes that Santorin could have caused not only Moses' three days of darkness but also parted the waters of

the Red Sea to allow the children of Israel to escape the pharoah's troops. When a
volcanic tidal wave (seismic sea wave) thunders down on a distant shore there is at first a
sucking back of the normal sea before it, leaving near the shore a dry area of sea bottom
for half an hour before the whole wave comes thundering back inland with a force that is
in proportion to the depth of the water. Krakatoa, the comparison blast of historic times
(1883) was in shallow water and the waves were 120 ft. high.

Santorin was in very deep water. This all points to a much bigger wave which further
substantiates the evidence that Atlantis disappeared with the eruption of Santorin. It
certainly explains several of our most miraculous Bible stories. A monstrous 200 ft. high
wave would have been traveling with such force (at least 350 miles per hour) that
Pharoah's soldiers would all have been drowned and tumbled miles inland along with
houses, trees, boats and anything else in its path. Krakatoa merely illustrates what must
have happened at "Atlantis" 3500 years before to say nothing of that entire part of the
ancient world.

Lest you think that volcanoes are all bad they also helped out on another Bible story
as Noah's Ark finally came to rest on Mt. Ararat, a 10,000 ft. volcano (still active) on the
Turkish-Armenian border. Sodom and Gomorrah are other volcanoes of the area that
erupted biblically in the cause of justice. Sodom and Gomorrah, cities of legendary
wickedness, were destroyed by a rain of "brimstone and fire" (Gen. 19:24). Their most
likely location is beneath the shallow waters at the southern end of the Dead Sea.

Bubbling Pools at Salton Sea: Here the liquid has the consistency of thick mud, and is a
good substitute for paint.

The Dead Sea Seen from the Judean Desert Mountains: The Dead Sea, the lowest spot
on Earth (1300 ft. below sea-level) is situated in the midst of a desolate wilderness.

From Santorin and Moses we jump over 3000 years to Ben Franklin and the French Revolution and their connection with another great world wide environmental influence from the Icelandic volcano Skaptor Jokel.

Benjamin Franklin, our first Ambassador to France, wrote about the unusual and devastating climate in May 1784. If not our first American volcanologist, Franklin was certainly the USA's first climatologist, in addition to everything else he discovered or invented. We quote him at length:

"During several summer months of the year 1783, when the effects of the sun's rays to heat the earth in these northern regions should have been greatest, there existed a constant fog over all of Europe and parts of North America. This fog was of a permanent nature; it was dry, and the rays of the sun seemed to have little effect in dissipating it as they easily do a moist fog rising from water. They were, indeed, rendered so faint in passing through it that, when collected in the focus of a burning glass they would scarcely kindle brown paper. Of course their summer effect in heating the earth was exceedingly diminished. Hence the surface was nearly frozen. Hence the snow remained on it unmelted and received continual additions… Perhaps the winter of 1783-84 was more severe than any that happened for many years."

Although Franklin and most of Europe knew of Iceland's great eruption, they did not put all the pieces together that their weather was a direct result of the volcano Skaptor Jokel. It was coupled with the volcano Asamayo in Japan the same year, one of several combination eruptions throughout the world which at various times have joined forces to effect the stratosphere.

Iceland had always plagued Europe, at least since the mid 12th century before Christ when the volcano Hekla (the back gate to Hell) blew millions of tons (several cubic miles) of dust particles into the atmosphere. The result caused 9% of the population of Scotland and northern England to migrate southward. This and subsequent eruptions from Iceland (Hekla around 207 B.C.) are preserved on ancient Chinese bamboo strips, although Iceland could have combined with some unknown Far Eastern eruption. Just as this dual volcanic force the same year was unbeknownst to Franklin, Chinese historians wrote of a great famine killing more than half the people. The harvest had failed for unknown reasons. The latter eruption has also been identified more recently by tree rings from Irish oaks and Greenland ice core samplings. Many of the famines in the Western world's Dark Ages are also attributable to Icelandic volcanoes.

CHAPTER IV

1783 LAKI
SKAPTOR JOKEL

"Let Them Eat Cake"
       – Marie Antoinette

"Let Them Eat Nothing"
       – The Volcano

It had never occurred to man until recently that volcanoes were responsible in large measure for the French Revolution in 1789. This historic revelation (the connection between climate change and politics) was first brought to our attention by Emmanuel LeRoy Ladore in his book *Times of Feast and Famine*, a fascinating study of climate and history. The great eruption of Laki, Skaptor Jokel, Iceland in 1783 caused climate conditions so bad all over Europe that the initial year of fresh snow in July was followed by five more severe winters and cold, soggy summers of crop failure and famine with no grain and no grape harvest summer after summer. By 1789 the desperate and angry populace stormed the Bastille, starting the French Revolution.

So enough about the world wide after effects, let's get to Iceland and its volcanoes and what they did and did not do for man in 1783, before and after.

"Amid the fires accumulates the snow, and frost remains where burning ashes glow; O'er ice eternal sweep the inactive flames, And winter, spite of fire, the region claims."
       – Claudian

Iceland, Land of Fire

In the cold North Atlantic is an amazing island 298 miles long and 194 miles wide composed entirely of lava but almost completely covered with snow and ice. This paradox of fire and frost was called Iceland by the Irish monk who where the island's first settlers before A.D. 800, but it could as well have been called Fireland.

Iceland (39,709 square miles) is about the size of Ohio, and the largest purely volcanic island in the world. It has 120 glaciers covering 107 volcanoes, more than 25 of them active in historic times. At least one of the volcanoes has erupted every 20 years since Eric the Red was Iceland's leader in 986. It was Lief, Eric's son, who discovered America 500 years before Columbus rediscovered it. Another Icelander, Thorfinn Karlsefni, established the first colony in "Vineland" (North America) about the year 1000, and his son Snorri was the first white man born in the new world. Both father and son returned to their strange homeland of steaming snowbanks and hot water glacier pools when their "Vineland" colony failed. Why the Icelanders preferred their volcanic ice pack to North America is anybody's guess.

Hostile Indians could scarcely have given them more trouble than the glaciers and volcanoes of their homeland. The whole business of Vikings crossing to North America does bring up one point, however. There have been several global coolings induced by volcano dust since the last Ice Age. One of these was The Dark Ages of Medieval times. It may have created enough polar ice to lower the North Atlantic Ocean just enough to have turned up many more islands, just as they may have lowered the water enough in the North Pacific to enable prehistoric man to cross the Bering Strait centuries earlier to populate North and South America with its native people.

The first Scandinavian who established permanent residence in Iceland was a rugged Norwegian named Ingolf Arnarson, who located his homestead there in 874 and called it Reykjavik. Reykjavik, the present capital of the kingdom, was selected like no other capital in the world.

Arnarson brought the main posts of his house from Norway on a Viking ship. When he reached the Icelandic coast he threw posts overboard and vowed to establish his new homestead wherever the posts washed ashore. Ashore they washed, and Reykjavik was started.

The first geysers were discovered in Iceland, and all geysers are named for "Geysir", the Icelandic region in which the hot water fountains were found and still boil out to this day.

There is a single snowfield in Iceland of 3000 square miles, and there are several over 500 miles. One glacier on the island is the size of Rhode Island, and there are 5,300 square miles covered constantly with blue glacial ice. Thirteen percent of the snow covered island is under glaciers, yet even these great ice fields cannot be considered permanent when the entire island under them is made of lava and honeycombed with active volcanoes. Volcanic activity has gone on continually since the island came above the water in a tertiary eruption fifty million years ago. Since the end of the last Ice Age, less than 500,000 years ago, 4,650 square miles of lava have welled up out of the earth to spill out on the island.

In the measurable period since 1500, Iceland has contributed one third of the world's new lava. There is no other (above sea level) area in the world where so many volcanoes are concentrated in such a small area. Yet it is not just this ever-threatening flow of lava which confronts Icelanders with their greatest hazard. The problem in this land of contrasts is not so much the red-hot lava as the snow it melts.

Icelandic hamlets cluster along narrow strips of seacoast pastureland, touched on the south shore by the warming Gulf Stream and offering a fish and flock economy.

Atop the Atlantic mid-ocean ridge (a volcanic island and submarine island chain) sits Iceland. We can only theorize on the cause (ocean spread, the earth's crust being thinner on the bottom of the ocean and/or the clash of tectonic plates) but the volcanoes are there well marked along the ridge built by volcanoes rising from the mid ocean trough. Beyond that we can only tell how and when they have erupted and speculate on why and when they will erupt again (every 20 years if the past is any guide to the future).

Many of Iceland's eruptions vomit lava straight out of the ground with no cone or crater. The earth opens up in a giant fissure and out pours the lava. Such was the case in 1783 at Skaptor Jokel (Laki) 80 miles east of Mt. Hekla, the always frightening "back gate to hell", where a 20 mile fissure opened up to boil lava out of 100 separate vents. *More lava flowed in this eruption than in any two others in world history.* The total content of lava vomited from this slit in the ground would form a mass larger than Pike's Peak. It continued to gush out of the ground for two years. The lava actually covered 218 square miles at an average depth of 100 feet.

In Skaptor Jokel (1783) the rugged people of Iceland and their island of fire and frost experienced the greatest volcanic eruption and catastrophe yet known to man. It completely dwarfed Vesuvius' greatest outburst in A.D. 79 and combined with Asamayama (Japan) the same year, causing world wide climate conditions that had doomsday predictions and political repercussions all over Europe.

Iceland's pending volcanic catastrophe, the greatest in the world up to that time, was ushered in towards the end of May, 1783 by a flourish of earthquakes of ever-increasing violence. The whole southern coast was violently agitated and a "new island" was raised 30 miles off the coast near Cape Reykianas and 200 miles from the unsuspected scene of devastation which followed. The island was christened Noye and claimed for the two-crowned King of Denmark and Iceland. This new possession of the dual monarchy was short lived. The volcanic force which created it transferred its attention to West Skaptorfell, on the main island of Iceland and left Noye to be eroded by the sea and reduced to an underwater shoal in less than a year.

By the first of June, citizens of West Skaptorfell, Syssel abandoned their dwellings because of the earthquakes and moved into tents. The bewildered population knew enough about volcanoes from Hekla's terrible eruption of 1755 and others in this fiery land to know that an eruption was foredoomed, but no one guessed from where or when the fateful explosion would come. On the eighth of June, their suspense was relieved, but not their fears.

Great pillars of smoke were seen rising from Laki on Skaptor Jokel which darkened the whole surrounding district and descended on the farms and villages in a whirlwind of ash and pumice. On the tenth of June, innumerable fountains of fire shot up through the snow which covered the mountain. It was an infernal fury which seemed to threaten the end of all things. Immense quantities of ice were melted, causing the rivers to overflow their banks. Down the Skaptor River Canyon flowed a swollen current of foul and poisonous water, but this too was short lived. A torrent of lava dispossessed the Skaptor of its bed, dammed up its source of supply and completely dried up the flooding river in less than 24 hours.

Lava streams from 22 different vents united to descend on the vast and deserted river gorge which was 200 feet wide and between 400 and 600 feet deep.

This grand canyon was entirely filled with red hot lava. It soon overflowed its sides to flood the surrounding country with an eerie sheet of uncompromising armor. It next ran into a deep lake which was quickly boiled dry in exploding steam. There followed a short respite as the lava took time to fill up the lake, after which the ever-flowing deluge disgorged itself on the lower fields of Medalland, wrapping this sizable district entirely in flames. Old lavas underwent fresh fusion or were ripped up and lacerated by the molten streams. Where the new lava could not melt old rock, it broke up the pieces and exploded them 150 feet into the air.

A second fissure of liquid fire vents opened eight days after the first to extend the volume and increase the fluidity of the lava flow to an eruption maximum of 100 spouts pouring from an open channel 20 miles long.

Having already filled a great lake and a 600-foot valley, it now pushed the river upstream toward the water's trouble source, but again the lava overflowed its banks. This time it was down a great waterfall where the water was pushed aside the astounding sight of a cataract of liquid fire. It quickly filled the abyss below the precipice and again overflowed the river banks to fan out on the plains like a spreading hand 12 to 15 miles wide and 100 feet thick. Houses crumbled in its path as the desolate river delta steamed and boiled as savagely as a new planet. A dog fell into the relentless lava flow and did not live long enough to yelp once. Other domestic animals left behind in locked barns bellowed their death cries above the explosive rumble of the approaching lava. At night the fresh lava had an amber glow.

The molten current, or currents (since there was flood upon flood of lava coming one on top of another) flowed for two months with ever-increasing fluidity and volume, but it had so far confined itself to the Skaptor river and surrounding country. The people of eastern Syssel, on the banks and delta of the Hverfisfloit River, lingered in hope that their lands and homes would escape complete destruction, although they were already buried in successive clouds of smoke and pumice. Showers of red-hot stones and ashes obliterated every vestige of vegetation and threatened the Syssel cattle with starvation, but the rugged farmers stuck to their homes. Then on August third, a thick stinking vapor rising from the river warned them of their coming doom. Having choked up all its Skaptor River outlets to the north and west, the liquid stone had swerved around the mountain and found the Hverfisfloit channel. The stream was speedily steamed dry making way for the foaming fiery flood of Skaptor Jokel to use the river bed. A blanket of fire soon ascended on to the plains where old lava flows melted and all combustible matter burned at its touch, thus giving the effect of the whole valley springing into flames.

Villages already buried under ash and then destroyed by floods of water and mud were now swallowed up by lava and entombed forever.

The two molten streams of lava quickly filled the deep river valleys that had taken water thousands of years to etch into Iceland's fire-rock lands. The lava then poured on into a boiling agitated sea. The Skaptor River flow was 50 miles long and 15 miles wide, with a maximum depth of 600 feet. The Hverfisfloit River branch was a lava flow 40 miles in length and seven miles wide. A still greater lava flood was heaped up in desolate areas around the base of Skaptor Jokel where no one lived to be dispossessed.

Altogether there were twenty towns and villages completely buried, and every inch of the great island was covered with pumice, sand and ashes. Dust from the eruption reached the Alps and obscured the sun over most of Europe.

The volcano went on vomiting lava for two years as the once rugged Norsemen were spasmodically showered in hot and cold water, mud, ash, and lava. Halfway through the eruption a Skaptor Jokel-inspired earthquake destroyed 100 additional Icelandic homes and damaged 400 more. The lava from this fantastic eruption was still steaming and giving off hot water 11 years after it poured out of the earth.

Noxious fumes asphyxiated man and beast alike and sulphuric ash destroyed vegetation all over the island so that 11,500 cattle, 28,000 horses and nearly 200,000 sheep died of starvation. This constituted three-fourths of the island's livestock population, 55 percent of the cattle, 77 percent of the horses and 82 percent of the sheep. 9,500 humans, or 20 percent of the island's people, also died in the flames and famine. Fish, the principal source of food, instinctively swam far out to sea to prevent their annihilation in the strange, hot water near the coast, and this added to the famine. Crops were destroyed in Scotland, 600 miles away, and plants were blighted by this supreme eruption in Holland, 1200 miles from Iceland.

In man's unnatural history, the inhuman suffering of 1783 did not belong exclusively to Iceland and Skaptor Jokel. It was also the year of the Calambria earthquake which killed 50,000 Italians, and of the tremendous volcanic eruption of Asamayama, which threw hotel-sized blocks of granite over the surrounding Japanese countryside.

It seems incredible to associate volcanic outbursts on opposite sides of the world, yet it must be more than coincidence that Skaptor Jokel, Asamayama and Calambria spelled out disaster in the same year, just as the 1902 series of eruptions would do 119 years later. If all this sounds like a scientist's theory on the birth of the planet earth, it at least manifests itself again every 100 years, and we could not realistically suppose that this century will be different. All man's misspent speculation about human causes affecting our environment are minuscule beside the real volcanic causes of these world wide natural disasters.

If further proof were needed to convince the suffering world of 1783 that there was an underworld connection joining the three catastrophes, they could recall events 28 years previous to Skaptor Jokel when the Lisbon earthquake of 1755 killed 60,000 people and left the Portuguese city a heap of ruins. The Lisbon earthquake was accompanied by earthquakes and volcanic outbursts which shook all of Europe and reverberated through the foundations of Asia, Africa and the Americas. Iceland marked 1755 with Hekla's greatest eruption, a disaster second in size and violence only to Skaptor Jokel in 1783. All of this Icelandic evidence of environmental changes is all the more evident because of Iceland's cultural and geographic ties to northern Europe. Certainly the effects of an Icelandic volcano show the folly the EPA ban on burning wood in your fireplace or not lighting your barbecue to cut down on smoke inhalation.

Skaptor Jokel's Plague (Laki)

Volcanic effects may be global, but the most dramatic events are still close to home. The aftermath is oftentimes worse than the eruption itself.

The plague of human suffering which followed in the wake of Skaptor Jokel's terrifying 1783 emissions is a horrible example of what the environment is up against when nature goes on a major rampage. This one is graphically described in William Hooker's 1809 account of Icelandic disease and pestilence during the winter and spring following the eruption of Skaptor Jokel in 1783.

"It was an epidemic distemper of a scorbutic and putrid nature accompanying the highest degree of cold-climate scurvy," said Hooker. "The scurvy broke out in sundry places, and among those persons even far distant from the fire. The district of West Skaptorfield was, however, the chief seat of this distemper; and in only six parishes there, no less than 150 persons were carried off. The same symptoms showed themselves in this disorder in the human race as among the cattle. The feet, thighs, hips, arms, throat and head were most dreadfully swelled, especially about the ankles, and knees and the various joints, which last, as well as the ribs, were contracted."

"The sinews, too, were drawn up with painful cramps, so that the wretched sufferers became crooked, and had an appearance the most pitiable. In addition to this, they were oppressed with pains across the breast and loins; their teeth became loose, and were covered with the swollen gums, which at length mortified and fell off in large pieces of a black or sometimes dark blue color."

"Disgusting sores were formed in the palate and throat, and not uncommonly at the extremity of the disease, the tongue rotted entirely out of the mouth. This dreadful, though apparently not very infectious distemper, prevailed in almost every farm in the vicinity of the fire during the winter and spring; but, happily, its extreme horrors were confined to the district of West Skaptorfield, beyond which it was attended with less melancholy."

"Many of the unfortunate inhabitants who resided in the vicinity of the place of eruption, and who could not procure either medicine or assistance, were starved to death; from an utter incapability of swallowing during the prevalence of the disorder, any portion of food, even if they could obtain it, which was not often the case. On the farm of Nupstad, in the Fliotshverfet, which was the only one of all that remained inhabited, till the spring of 1784, the distemper attacked every individual among the inhabitants, not leaving a single person in health to assist and comfort the sick with the necessary attendance. Report goes even so far as to state that several persons had been lying dead in their houses for a considerable time, before any intelligence of their decease could reach Siden, the nearest station; and that the information was at length conveyed by some travelers from the east country, who accidentally stopped at Nupstad, and there heard from the few survivors of the distressing situation of the district."

"Both there and at Horgsland and, indeed at some other places, it was necessary to burn the bodies upon the spot; since there were no horses left and but few persons who were able to convey the deceased to the church. I ought indeed to add that the circumstance of the earth being frozen to a considerable depth, as well during the spring as the winter of 1784, made a measure of this kind more indispensable; the few that were free from disease being so enfeebled by hunger, that they had by no means strength sufficient to break up the indurated ground and open graves for so great a number of bodies as now required interment."

"As often, therefore, as burial was at all resorted to, six, seven, eight and even ten bodies were placed in one grave and, for the sake of sparing exertions that they were little able to encounter, this was frequently so shallow as barely to allow a covering of earth above the lid of the coffin. That the air from such a mode of interment must soon become corrupted and dangerous for the human race, especially in the summer season, is a fact that speaks for itself."

"It is necessary for me here to remark that the disorder principally attacked those who had previously suffered from want and hunger and who had protracted a miserable existence by eating the flesh of such animals, not even excepting horses, as had died of the same distemper and by having recourse to boiled skins and other most unwholesome and indigestible food. I have been assured by survivors in the district of Skaptorfield that the flesh and milk of sick animals had a remarkably unpleasant taste and that, in particular, the milk was of an unusually dark and yellow color."

"From respect to my readers I forbear to enumerate a variety of other things which, as articles of food, were in an equal or greater degree nauseous and disgusting and which, were I to detail them, would serve to show what shocking expedients the extreme cravings of appetite will drive men to have recourse to, and how it is possible to convert almost everything to food."

"Some of the inhabitants, during the whole course of the winter, had not the least morsel of any kind of fresh or wholesome victuals, nor were they able to procure any other beverage than the water which had been corrupted by the mixture of ashes and sulphur-dust. It was not all, however, even in this case, who died, but some recovered after having, in the course of the following summer, a fresh supply of cows and some provisions conveyed to them from the sea coast. After the pastures once more afforded them their wanted supply, being again covered with good grass and herbage, things improved greatly. Various kinds of sorrel and dandelion were picked from which the hungry natives made spoon bread."

There is little doubt that the eruptions of 1783 caused world wide air pollution and resulting suffering. No one who endured could predict that things could and would be even worse within many of the survivor's lifetimes when the single volcano, Tambora, threw out as much global air pollutants as Asamayama and Skaptor Jokel-Laki combined.

Japan's Asamayama in 1783 tossed out the biggest boulder (264 x 120 ft) yet recorded by a volcano, the huge block of lava landed in a river and was charted as a new island. Asamayama erupted the same year as Skaptor Jokel (Iceland) and led scientists to speculate what global effects could occur if several volcanoes erupted the same year.

CHAPTER V

1815 TAMBORA – RECORDED HISTORY'S MOST VOLUMINOUS AIR POLLUTER

Just 32 years after the volcanoes Skaptor Jokel and Asamayama had created the conditions which ultimately caused the French Revolution, a volcano was back to haunt Europe again. This time it was Tambora on the island of Sumbawa in far off Indonesia. One volcano erupting 50 cubic miles of air pollutants to "strat load" the globe's upper air currents and obscure the normal summer sun's warmth.

The eruption started April 5, 1815, but the climate effects in Europe and North America where not apparent for almost a year. 1816 was labeled "the year without a summer" and 1817-1819 "summers" were not much better.

The period was marked by the end of the Napoleonic era, but neither Napoleon (safely tucked away on the volcanic island of St. Helena by 1815) nor the reactionary Austrian Count Von Metternich, whose political influence dominated Europe in the period just after the Napoleonic wars, could have caused what the historian J.W. Post calls "the last great subsistence crises in the Western World." The years 1816, 1817, 1818 and 1819 produced almost complete crop failure, the potato famine and political unrest all over Europe and much of northeastern North America.

To recite a few of the conditions:

Thousands of desperate hollow eyed, sallow cheeked beggars swarmed every highway like a rag tag army begging for food, any food at all. There was snow in every month and frost never left the ground during the usual growing months of May through October. It rained constantly, and what crops started, rotted in the ground. There was no grape harvest in France for several years and once again, the French government was overthrown. Troops were constantly on guard against their own people all over Europe. The suicide rate was the highest it had or has been to this day, and criminal activity in places like Switzerland replaced a normally peace loving society. The first anti-Semitic race riots began in Germany as hungry people somehow blamed the Jews. At Lord Byron's villa in Switzerland, Mary Shelly was inspired to write her gory novel, *Frankenstein*. A wave of arson followed food riots in Holland, Belgium and France. In New England experienced a huge migration westward all over the northeastern U.S. and

Eastern Canada, there was widespread snow in June and frost continued into July, August and September. Corn was knee high by September fourth, but not by the usual fourth of July. The old Farmer's Almanac, through a mistake in proofreading, had predicted snow for July in 1816 and has ever after been a source of weather prediction that old timers have faith in. This was what happened throughout the world. So what happened in southeast Asia due to the volcanoes there?

Terrible Tom, The Assassin of Sumbawa

Sumbawa is a medium-sized island (5,965 square miles) in a volcanic chain running from Australia to Asia. It lies between the Flores Sea and the Indian Ocean, three islands south of Java. The principal crops are rice, corn and tobacco. In the spring of 1815, Sumbawa was a British possession with 13,000 foot Tambora Mountain its principal landmark. Peaceful Tambora on the northside of the island was a volcano, but it had not erupted in the memory of man. All this was prior to April 5th, when the size and shape of the mountain and of the entire island changed in the most violent explosion on record up to that time and ever since.

Terrible Tom threw so much dirt into the stratosphere that the sun which never sets on the British Empire was seen only through a dry fog in the summerless year which followed the colossal blast. The average world temperature was reduced by two degrees for the entire year.

Volcanologists disagree on how much material was ejected by the volcano, but they all agree that no eruption in modern historic times (since we kept records) has come close to the amount of rock, ash and fine dust plus all the environmental gases (CO_2, SO_2, chlorine and H_2O) blown sky high from its crater during ten explosive days. Verbeek estimates the ejected material to exceed 36 cubic miles and Junghuhn places the quantity at 93 cubic miles. Other estimates ranged between these two extremes and averaged upward of 50 cubic miles. This means the explosion was at least 200 times more devastating than St. Helens 1981 in amount ejected.

Difficulties in measuring the amount of rock, dirt, dust and sand, some of which stayed suspended in the air for a year and gases for much longer (up to seven years), are understandable, but there are numerous phenomena of Terrible Tom's greatest outburst which are measured fact. The explosion was heard in Sumatra, 970 miles distant, in a blast so great that it shook the ground from Java to Borneo, a distance of more than 1000 miles. Ash was blown so high that it was carried counter-monsoon to Banda 800 miles away. Ash fall was two feet thick, 850 miles from the explosion and dust was dropped over a million square miles. Finer particles stayed suspended in the atmosphere for more than two years. Parts of Java, 300 miles from Sumbawa, were in total darkness for three days. The lava from Skaptor Jokel, the greatest historic measured eruption before Terrible Tom, would make one Pike's Peak. Tambora's outlay of sand, ash, dust and lava would be enough for three such mountains. Skaptor's lava flow would seal Texas under a sheet of armor; Tom would bury the Lone Star State under two feet of ash. Nine thousand five hundred people were killed by Skaptor Jokel. Terrible Tom, located in a much more heavily populated area, snuffed out 56,000 lives.

Tambora, like Krakatoa 68 years later, was too powerful for the survival of close-in eye witnesses. Most of the existing accounts concern measurements of the quantity of rock and ash it exploded, the distance at which the explosion was heard and the fantastic numbers killed and property devastated by the eruption in areas far removed from the origin of the explosion.

According to the after-action report of Sir Stamford Raffles, British Governor-General of Sumbawa, there were no fewer than 12,000 individuals in the provinces of Tambora and Pekate at the time of the eruption and only six persons survived. Of all the villages around the volcano, only Temp, population 40, escaped annihilation. At Sangir, a larger island port adjoining Sumbawa, ships could not plow through the floating pumice which was several feet thick. All crops were destroyed and buried three feet deep on Sangir Island as rooftops collapsed under the weight of "the night of ash". The famine occasioned by this event was so extreme that one of the Rajah's own daughters died of starvation.

Ashes two feet thick covered the entire island of Tombock, more than 100 miles distant, and 44,000 persons perished by starvation after the total destruction of all domestic animals and edible vegetation.

The main eruption of Terrible Tom lasted only ten days, beginning April 5th and ending April 14th, 1815. During this period the 13,000 foot mountain reduced itself to 9,000 feet and left a hole seven miles in diameter and 425 feet deep where the missing 4,000 foot mountain top had once been. The remains of the missing mountain were exploded in fragments ranging in blocks from box-car size and larger to a fine powder. Combined with new lava blown out of the center of the earth, the mountain of material ejected was estimated at more than fifty cubic miles.

This colossal eruption of Terrible Tom was preceded by six months of small ash explosions and was followed by two months of declining intensity, but the main attack began on April 5th, and exploded every 15 minutes until the climax blast on the night of April 10th, during which the whole mountain top collapsed. Before the volcano began smoking in 1813, it was considered extinct.

For the full account of the eruption chronology we again go to Sir Stamford Raffles, who observed the eruption from Sangir:

"(On April 5th) the whole mountain appeared like a body of liquid fire extending itself in every direction. This fire and columns of flame continued to rage with unabated fury until obscured by complete darkness behind a blanket of ash."

"Stones fell thick at Sangir, some of them as large as two fists but most no larger than walnuts. Between 9:00 and 10:00 p.m. ashes fell and a violent whirlwind ensued which blew down nearly every house and carried away roofs and light parts. The largest trees were torn up by the roots and carried into the air together with men, horses, cattle and whatsoever came within its influence. This would account for the immense number of trees later seen floating at sea."

"The sea rose twelve feet higher than its previous height at highest storm-tide, spoiling the rice lands and sweeping away all houses within its reach."

"The whirlwind lasted about an hour and no explosions were heard until it ceased about 11:00 p.m. But from midnight of the 5th until the 11th of April, they continued without intermission and after that at intervals until the 15th of July. Sounds like gunfire from the April 5th explosions were heard on a neighboring island and troops were dispatched to look for pirates. They returned three days later with no pirates but reports of a great new volcano that had already covered Sumbawa with ash."

No noise up to that time was ever so loud or heard so far away as Terrible Tom's 1000-mile record the night of April 10th. Only Krakatoa has since topped Tambora's loudest roar with a phenomenal blast in 1883. Since no one was alerted to listen for a night-time volcano blast, sound from the explosion may have carried much farther than the 970 miles recorded in Sumatra and the 7200 mile "cannon shot" reported by a fisherman in Ternate.

A compressed pint of Tambora's fine powder-like ash weighs twelve and three-quarter ounces, according to Dr. Jagaar. In quantity this ash dust had sufficient weight to break down houses at Bima, a Sumbawa port city 40 miles away from the crater. It also made the houses uninhabitable as the fine particles penetrated rugs, linen, clothing; everything not already collapsed or buried. Boats were driven ashore by the agitated seas, and water a foot deep entered the houses to make an ash paste of the volcanic powder. Floating pumice two feet thick and miles across obstructed shipping in vast areas west of Java.

At Tambora peninsula, there was an 18-foot lowering of the land as if to compensate for the underground hollow left by the tremendous quantities of stone blown out of the volcano. This land was still under water 165 years after the eruption.

The explosion on the night of April 10th was accompanied by a 14-foot tidal wave. it is estimated that 10,000 people were killed in that first night in this thinly populated area by falling rocks, streams of glowing lava, blasts of suffocating ash-filled air, or by drowning in the sea. Four times this many later died from starvation and dysentery, as falling ash choked the life from crops and polluted drinking water. Sumbawa's 6,000 square miles were entirely devastated as its cattle died, and its rice, corn and sugar cane were destroyed. The island is 165 miles long and 60 miles wide, yet every inch of it felt the effects of the eruption in some horrible way. Most of the island's 300,000 people were temporarily evacuated. People on nearby islands were equally hard-pressed and miserable for more than two years after the disaster first struck them down.

The far-flung effects of Tom's terrible temper were felt on April 11th when houses in Java were violently jerked. Persons throughout the East Indies reported a repeated jarring motion of the ground with a weird subterranean rattling and rumbling. Ships were capsized and grounded by earthquake flood waves as the volcano shook the whole East Indies area in its rage.

Measured in quantity of materials displaced from the earth, blown into the air and spread around the world, the 1815 eruption of Terrible Tom was, and still is, the world's greatest explosion. Although the volcano's blast was neither so loud nor so powerful as the eruption of Krakatoa, its more famous neighbor 68 years later, the volcanic output was perhaps 20 times as great as that of Krakatoa. Only the legendary Santorin may have exceeded both Tambora in volume of materials thrown out and Krakatoa in explosive power. It certainly had even more influence on the roots of western culture.

Aerial view of Tambora volcano in Indonesia: neither sunspots nor lightning rods.

In effects on the climate, the ejecta from Tambora was not as well recorded as Krakatoa 68 years later. Few knew what was causing their discomfort, but discomfort was noted half way around the world in Concord, New Hampshire on June 6, 1816 where one of the guests at the inauguration of Governor William Plumber complained that "our teeth chattered in our heads and our feet and hands were benumbed." In Lord Byron's Swiss Villa on the shore of Lake Geneva, the chill and rain confined guests to his villa where they amused themselves with climate induced ghostly tales. Mary Shelly's became the basis for her novel *Frankenstein*.

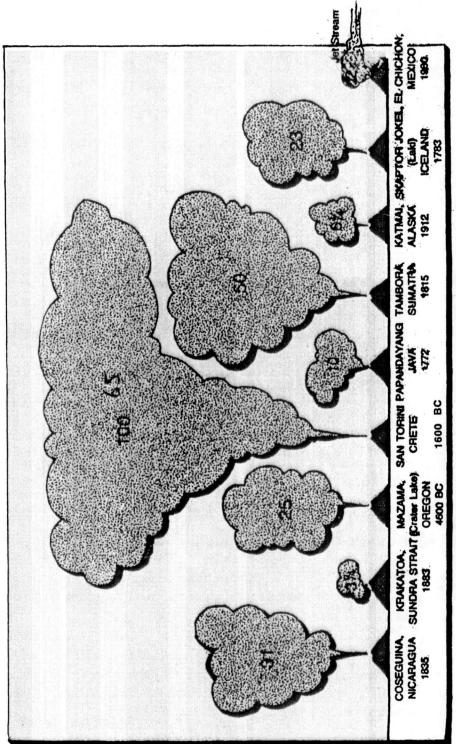

THE BIGGIES - Volume of Material Ejected (in cubic miles)

Volcanoes & Religion – Why Not?

"Frankly, I don't take much stock in this business of the gods being angry. The way I got it doped out is that at great depths the heat caused by the enormous pressure of the earth's crust melts the stone and turns some of it into gases. See? Then you got down there a vapor tension strong enough to blow the whole works to the surface, providing, of course, a channel of weakness opens up for it."

Drawing by Garrett Price; Copyright © 1945 The New Yorker Magazine, Inc.

CHAPTER VI

KRAKATOA
NOISE POLLUTION –
EARTH'S BIGGEST BANG!!
THE BIG VOLCANO SOUND WAS OVER 100 YEARS AGO

"I hear your rumble volcano."

On August 27, 1883, Krakatoa erupted with a blast three times as loud as any noise man has ever heard. Imagine a sound being picked up by the naked ear at Rodriquez Island in the Indian Ocean, 3,000 miles from the eruption's blast four hours earlier! A coast guardsman and the chief of police, mistaking the sound for navel gunfire just offshore, mobilized their people to defend the island against attack.

Sound "like the firing of heavy artillery" was the way shepherds on the Victoria Plains of West Australia, 1700 miles from Krakatoa, described the blast. At Day Waters, South Australia, 2023 English miles away, townsfolk were aroused by what they thought was "the blasting of rock which lasted several minutes." In the British Chagos Islands in the Indian Ocean 2167 miles from the volcano, natives heard "thundering noises" and thought "a ship must be in distress."

At Singapore, 500 miles away, an operator at the Oriental Telephone Company put the receiver to her ear and heard "a roar like a waterfall." At Ishore a receiver on a line from the submarine cable sounded like "pistol shots."

In Java and Sumatra, 100 miles distant, a continuous and deafening roar hammered every eardrum to the bursting point for two days.

The "monster's voice" was also heard in the streets of Bangkok, 1413 miles; the Philippines 1450 miles; and Ceylon, 2058 miles from its origin and it would have been heard at even greater distance if people had been warned to listen the way they are reminded to watch for an eclipse.

Imagine an explosion in New York City so loud that it would keep you awake all night in Philadelphia and be observed without benefit of hearing aid by people in Los Angeles, London, Havana, Brownsville, Texas and St. Paul, Minnesota. This was the power of Krakatoa whose sound and air waves girdled the globe binding it like a noisey mummy.

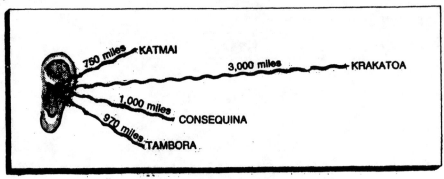

Distance Heard by Human Ear

The Jet Stream (Volcanic Version)

"Had the fierce ashes of some fiery Peak been hurled so high they
ranged around the globe? For day by day through many a blood-red eve
the wrathful sunset glared..."
(From Alfred Lord Tennyson's "St. Telemachus")

Krakatoa, by throwing 3 1/2 cubic miles of dust and debris as much as 20 miles above earth's surface, gave us our first knowledge of the jet stream turbulence which circles the globe above the ten-mile limit. These special winds, traveling about twice the speed of an express train, in 1883 carried Krakatoa's volcanic ash around the world in 13 days and then made the trip six more times for good measure, as its dust stayed aloft, suspended in the stratosphere for two years.

A cubic mile of heavier rock was broken up and scattered over an area equal to all the New England states plus New York, New Jersey, Pennsylvania, Ohio, Indiana and Illinois (284,170 square miles) in a gravel storm of subterranean top soil. Ships 1600 miles from the eruption were covered with ashes three days after the explosion.

The prodigious quantities of microscopic dust particles ground up by Krakatoa's explosion and shot into the stratosphere spun a veil of material denying normal visibility to hundreds of cubic miles of air. Pyrheliometric observations, measuring the amount of the sun's heat to reach earth's surface, found it only 87% normal in the year following the eruption. Try to visualize this explosion, so profound as to reduce our effective sunlight 13% throughout the world for a full year.

Krakatoa turned the sun blue and green all day and turned the moon and stars green at night as far away as Ceylon and San Salvador. In Paris, New York, Cairo and London, for many months after the eruption the setting sun appeared blue, leaden, green and copper-colored with a rainbow colored sky.

There is no doubt Krakatoa traveled the world's jet stream 50 years before man built the first jet and over 100 years before man arrogantly began speculating that he could control global air pollution by regulating the burning of fossil fuels.

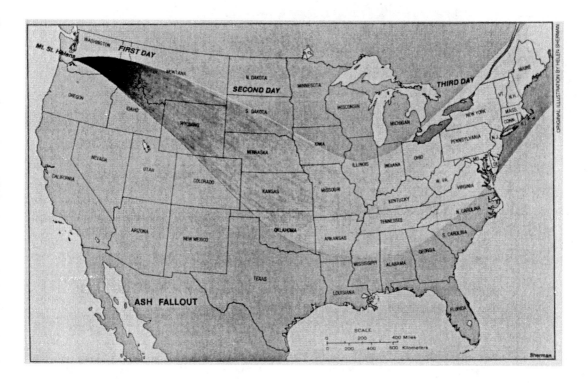

1883-1981 Ninety eight years later. A lesson learned from Krakatoa. Ashfall from St. Helen's is plotted as the jet stream carries it across North America.

KRAKATOA, MORE POWERFUL THAN ONE-HUNDRED H-BOMBS

Krakatoa was clearly the loudest and noisiest volcano heard by man. As far as the power of it's explosion it may have been the most measured.

On March 1, 1954, the United States detonated an H-Bomb 600 times more powerful than the Hiroshima A-Bomb, dubbing the monster "Ivy." This "peacetime test" was equivalent to 12 to 14 million tons of TNT (more than all the bombs we dropped in World War II) in a blast so powerful it critically burned Japanese fishermen on a vessel at least 70 miles away – fishermen who described the explosion as "brighter than the sun" and "like many thunders rolled into one."

These facts and figures astonished attending scientists, yet compared with nature's loudest blast at Krakatoa in 1883, "Ivy's" tests were very small explosions.

Krakatoa was an uninhabited island in the Sundra Straits between Java and Sumatra. One might call it a brooding monster but it had not brooded enough to erupt for 200 years nor was there any way of anticipating it would again. Then on Sunday, 26 August 1883, it began a series of explosions culminating the next morning in a gigantic spasm which blew three islands to bits, leaving a hole 1000 feet deep in the ocean where a mountain 2600 feet high had stood. This void would hold not 14 pentagon buildings, as would the H-Bomb crater under "Ivy", but 340. Whereas "Ivy" had one water spout, Krakatoa had 15. No eyewitness could have lived through Krakatoa and fortunately none were around, but results were so decisive that even at great distance observers labeled it the most powerful explosion of all time.

Four Ships Survived

The post-World War II underwater A-bomb explosions at Bikini (not to be confused with the 1954 H-bomb air bursts there), destroyed only five of the "planted" naval vessels. The battleship Nevada, 300 to 500 yards from point zero, was but partially damaged.

Ships on the sea seem to be able to roll better with the punch of an atomic - or volcanic - tidal wave then can nearby shore installations. Such was the case of Krakatoa, which sent a man-of-war two miles inland with anchor dragging and left it stranded high on a jungle hill, while four merchant ships, the "Charles Ball," the "Sir R. Sale," the "G.G. London," and the "Northern Castle" survived between 10 and 50 miles away from Krakatoa to bring back the only vague record of what the eruption looked like.

All day August 27th, the four helpless vessels lay in total darkness under a rain of stone, bobbing like singed corks in an oatmeal sea.

Two miles from the explosion, Verlaten Island was covered with a layer of ashes 100 feet thick. The formerly fertile and densely populated islands of Sibuku and Sibesi, ten and 15 miles away, were entirely covered by mud several yards thick and all inhabitants perished. Red-hot debris was thrown over an area the size of Germany and, despite the fact that there were no large towns within 100 miles, 36,000 persons were swept to watery graves.

Yet only ten sea miles away the British ship "Charles Ball" survived – although no one on board expected to live through the barrage. Stones the size of men's skulls cannonaded the ship further drenched with phosphorescent mud-rain full of pumice and evil-smelling sulphur. "Chains of fire seemed to be ascending between the volcano and the sky and a continual roll of white, incandescent balls rolled down the sides of the mountain."

Captain Wooldrige, of the "Sir R. Sale," wrote in his ship's log, "the volcano appears as an immense pine tree silhouetted in a black mass with its stem and branches formed by lightning bolts." The Roman sailor named Pliny had described Vesuvius just that way in 79 A.D.

The "Northern Castle," 30 miles out in this volcanic purgatory, reported "iron-cinder masses hurtling through the air and hot, choking air that smelled of sulphur and burning clinkers." The captain described the sight before him as looking like an "immense wall with blazing serpents running over it." Later, when bursts of forked lightning vanished, it appeared as "a blood-red curtain bordered in yellow."

In sounding the lead from a bottom of thirty fathoms, a sailor aboard the "G.G. London," 50 miles from Krakatoa, reported "It came up warm." Millions of dead fish lay belly-up over the Sundra Straits.

These are the best we have of Krakatoa's eyewitness accounts. It was an explosion so intense no one lived long enough and close enough to tell us much about it. That 27 August, 1883, perhaps the hottest day in recorded time since it was the day hell came closest to escaping its subterranean cell, must be measured in terms of distant effects. The last man to set foot on Krakatoa was a Dutch captain named Ferzenaar, who reported the ground so hot it burned right through the soles of his boots. This was more than three weeks before Krakatoa's August 27th volcanic D-day.

Post-Log... Krakatoa

Just before the remains of Krakatoa completely vanished behind its ebony smoke curtain at 10:20 Sunday morning, 27 August 1883, sailors on the "Charles Ball" saw the entire island (nine square miles) rocket skyward and disappear in its 17 mile penetration of space. They did not know it until much later, but three islands disappeared, and where Krakatoa had been one-half mile high there was now a hole in the ocean 1000 feet deep.

The combination of lava bursting out and the ocean rushing in turned the sea to boiling steam whenever it hit the volcano's burning interior. This happened again and again as ocean and lava battled, sending enormous blocks of granite to rocket skyward in the resulting cataclysm.

The ocean finally won out when water reached the volcano's core. In one final seizure the heart was ripped out of Krakatoa and like the burst shell casing on an atomic missile, the whole island was pulverized and two others were blown up with it.

Krakatoa was complete desolation. Most of the island had disintegrated in the blast and the rest was a lifeless mass of rock buried under a mountain of ashes. Every plant, animal, insect or bird had been cremated in the volcano's fiery cloud, yet there was an aftermath. Seeds dropped by birds, eggs, worms and larvae floated in from the sea; the wind blew in spiders, caterpillars, beetles and butterflies.

There was an evolution chronology of life telescoping millenniums into months. Some forms of life were necessary so that others could survive, while still others threatened to over-run the place until their natural enemies appeared.

By 1910 it was swarms of ants. By 1920 birds and reptiles had all but eliminated the ants. Trees began in 1919 and became a young forest by 1924. In a few more years vines and creepers took on the trees. Krakatoa became a laboratory for life instead of death. It was a naturalist's paradise protected as such by Dutch law, and men of science used it to record the development of life. Even volcanoes cannot snuff out the miracle of life. Always it will reappear in some form.

Krakatoa showed signs of renewed activity in January, 1928. By the summer of 1930 a new crater rose out of the sea a short distance from the island. Termed Anak ('Baby') Krakatoa, it is a certain sign that the forces which actuated Krakatoa are not sleeping too deeply, but in the meantime life goes on.

The Sea Waves of Krakatoa

The most astounding results of the 1883 eruption of the volcano Krakatoa were not in the air or on the ground, but in the ocean where 36,000 people were drowned in seismic sea waves (tidal waves) of enormous height and length.

Fortunately, Krakatoa was a long way from the United States or your living room in Los Angeles or the East Coast might have been full of water and your house washed away if it were less than 50 feet above sea level.

Unable to inflict mass human suffering in the normal volcanic ways (poison gas, hot lava, raining stones and mud avalanches) because it was in a remote area, Krakatoa took its toll indirectly through the sea. Several tidal waves from 50 to 150 feet high were generated by the explosion. They swept over Java and Sumatra at a speed of nearly 400 miles per hour, destroying 1,000 seaside villages and grounding vessels hundreds of miles away. Large ships were carried miles off their course at an equivalent distance from New York to the Panama Canal. Houses 50 feet above sea level disappeared completely and were never seen again.

In the Sundra Straits the resistless fury of the waves was such that they tore 50-ton chunks of coral out of their sea beds and rolled them inland like snowballs. A wave 135 feet high engulfed the village of Merak, 33 miles from the volcano, and left nothing in its wake.

A mere 50 miles away in Anjer, Reverend Philip Neal described it like this: "Looking out to sea in the heavy volcanic overcast that had descended on everything that memorable Sunday, Neal thought he saw a new island rising out of the ocean. It seemed like a low range of hills but a closer squint convinced him it was a lofty ridge of black water racing toward him at great speed. He turned and ran for high ground but not soon enough. A 50 foot wall of water engulfed the town, battering down everything in its way.

One second Neal heard the resistless mass of water behind him and the next he was knocked out by the rushing torrent and swept inland. When he came to, the preacher was sitting on top of a palm tree, stunned and stripped of his vestments but otherwise unharmed. Why his tree had stood while most of the others were uprooted and thrown down he didn't know.

The huge wave rolled on, gradually decreasing in height and strength until it reached the mountain slopes behind Anjer. Then, its fury spent, the water gradually receded and flowed back into the sea. As Neal clung to his palm tree, wet and exhausted, there floated past the dead bodies of his friends and neighbors. Only a handful of the population escaped. Houses and streets were completely destroyed, and scarcely a trace remained of where the thriving town once stood.

Dead bodies, fallen trees, wrecked houses, an immense muddy morass, pools of water and the Reverend Neal were all that was left of Anjer."

Long waves from Krakatoa lapped the shores of five continents. They reached Cape Horn, 7813 miles from point center, and the English Channel, 11,040 miles away from the eruption. Another of the seismic sea waves from the explosion was still 18 inches high when it reached Table Bay, West Africa, 5100 miles from its origin.

Everywhere within a 100 mile radius of Krakatoa there was a five-foot layer of pumice on the sea. Navigation was like plowing through an ice flow or a pot of porridge. Great quantities of Krakatoa's floating ash were washed up at Tamatave, Madagascar (5800 miles away) a year later.

Fifty miles from the explosion there were 15 simultaneous water spouts being sucked into the heavens within the vision of one terrified sailor aboard the ship, "G.G. London," and he noted a peculiar pinkish flame coming from the clouds. "It looked as if balls of fire studded the masthead and yardarms." The mainmast conductor was struck by lightning six times and the mud-rain which covered the rigging, decks and masts was phosphorescent and presented the appearance of St. Elmo's fire. The native crew were so frightened by these "evil spirits" that they staged a sit-down strike while the ship floundered in the turbulent ash-covered sea.

Krakatau's 'warning' eruption in May 1883; no one got a picture of the big blast the following August.

The Caldera Theory of a mountaintop collapsing into the volcano when molten magma has eaten away its underpinnings, began with the study of Krakatoa (1883). St. Helens (for instance) which was more powerful than Mexico's El Chichón (about one year later) had no such influence on climate because El Chichón's jungle covered top collapsed completely into the volcano, like a huge cannon being muzzle loaded (caulked and charged) before a blast. The combined accumulation of stratospheric dust ejected from St. Helens and El Chichón the same year contributed to deflection of the sun in a manner similar to but far smaller and much less dramatic than Krakatoa. Most of the great air polluting eruptions were these Caldera type explosions from Crater Lake, Oregon in prehistoric times to Santorin, Greek Islands 1600 B.C. to Tambora 1815 to Krakatoa, Katmai, Alaska (1912) and on to El Chichón, Mexico in 1981. All of these loaded the stratosphere with pollutants many times as great as any insignificant polluting many is capable of doing. His puny efforts have never added up to more than three percent of the overall total of air pollutants.

A gas exploded cloud of flaming sand soared down the mountain to the sea, blasting over and incinerating a whole town and all its 30,000 people in six seconds.

St. Pierre, Martinique, May 8, 1902

CHAPTER VII

THE MARTINIQUE HORROR AT THE DOOMED CITY OF ST. PIERRE

"This date should be written in blood..."

M. Gabriel Parel
Vicar-General of Martinique

The beautiful city of St. Pierre, Martinique was called "the Pearl of the Lesser Antilles." Here, at last, was the sublime dream of the weary traveler, a travel folder paradise of gentle tropic climate, blue sea lapping at sun-drenched beaches, gaily dressed and singing Creole beauties with a kindly old volcano affectionately called "Old Uncle Pipe Smoker" as a scenic backdrop. A waft of morning breeze flowed over the flowers and trees and fountains, and over the green parks and red tile roofs. It was peaceful, comfortable, clean and not expensive.

Columbus discovered Martinique in 1502. It has 400 mountains, 380 square miles and 6000 more women than men. It is the most beautiful and romantic island in the West Indies. The Empress Josephine was born there; it was the favorite hunting ground of Lord Nelson; Mme de Maintenon flowered into womanhood there, and Aimee Dubois left the island via shipwreck, piracy and the slave market to become consort of one Sultan and mother of another.

Martinique is an island of contrasts in wealth and poverty, but its riot of vegetation, productive soil and a sea alive with food, leave everyone carefree and well fed. It is French and has been since 1635 when King Louis XIII established the colony at St. Pierre.

St. Pierre is or was 1,710 miles from New York City (closer than Denver, Colorado) on the windward passage of the Caribbean. And unlike the previous eruptions described in this book, this ultimate tragedy was not ancient history but in the 20th century. This beautiful city sat like an island rock garden on the lower slopes of Mt. Pelee, a 4,430 foot active volcano five miles away, whose crater, prior to April 1902, housed a beautiful mountain lake surrounded by ferns and lobelia. Romantics in St. Pierre used to climb the volcano's green shoulders to swim in the crater and picnic in the shaded forests beside it. The town by 1902 was wealthy and very gay.

Among the 30,000 Pierrotins were probably 8,000 white Creoles, a close-knit society sophisticated and thoroughly French, who controlled the wealth not only the commercial city of St. Pierre but all of Martinique. Conservative in politics, they were Gaulically liberal in their lifestyle so that St. Pierre was also known as the lustiest port in the already-heady Caribbean.

And then in a mere six seconds on Fiesta Day of May 8, 1902, all of this was gone. Thirty thousand souls were hurled into eternity in an avalanche of fire that turned the city into one big charnel house. Every living thing was dead, every tree was torn up by the roots or snapped off at the stump, every building was flattened with gasses burning on the stone-walled wreckage much like a flame thrower licking a pill box with fire. Everything went, as dry stubble before the sweep of a prairie blaze. The hurricane of flame was so sudden that no person lived long enough to take two steps toward escape and not more than one breath of the fire gas. Many bodies were cauterized from within while their clothes remained on their bodies. A whole city had been cremated, from cats and dogs to cathedral bells melting as they sobbed their death toll. The volcano warred on demon rum with gaping holes in the quarter inch iron distillery tanks which looked as if they were punched with a high-velocity anti-tank gun. St. Pierre's own heavy cannon were torn from their mountings in the fort above the city. Even the sea hissed and shrank back. Thirty seconds after the wall of flame swept through St. Pierre, a dense cloud brought complete darkness, a blackout on its own unprecedented destruction. No one lived to ask why the volcano they loved had done this to them. The wall of fry gas shot down the mountain covering the six miles in six seconds.

Sir Bulwar Lytton's *Last Days of Pompeii* exaggerates the public horrors in the AD 79 eruption of Vesuvius, but the novel seems understated when compared with the last six seconds of St. Pierre in 1902. Like Vesuvius, the volcano Pelee, which had not erupted since 1851, gave ominous warning for a month before the 1902 disaster. But local authorities as well as the populace were chiefly concerned with the forthcoming elections. The Governor of Martinique arrived from Fort de France to reassure the people and insure a good turnout at the polls. When disaster finally struck, after repeated warnings were ignored, it destroyed every thing and every body. The governor, the candidates, the voters, the proclamations and even the ballots all were burned beyond recognition. The only survivor in down town St. Pierre was the defranchised black prisoner, Auguste Ciparis, found four days later in his subterranean cell by French sailors from a rescue party off the warship *Surchet* sent in to assess the devastation. Ciparis was pardoned for his crime later and became a minor celebrity as a sideshow attraction with Barnum & Bailey Circus (exhibiting his scars).

It all started very early on the morning of May 8, 1902 in an underground prison in St. Pierre, Martinique. Auguste Ciparis, the sole prisoner, stirred, opened his eyes and got up from the plain plank which served as a bed. Ciparis was feeling very sorry for himself, for in three days, came Election Day. As he had been de-franchised, Auguste could not vote even if he were free, but he really didn't mind that part. What annoyed him was that Election meant Fiesta, and Auguste had already spent a month in the underground cell, far removed from the swaying hips and suggestive glances of St. Pierre's devilishly attractive mulatto girls (a blend of Carib Indian, French and Negro).

The day before, on the 7th day of May, the ships of the U.S. Navy had sailed away with 2000 sailors who had spent four days tasting the delights of this "Pearl of the Lesser Antilles." American sailors in town always meant fun and extra money for Auguste, and this time he hadn't made a penny from the free-spenders. St. Pierre, with its 118 rum distilleries and what were reputed to be the most beautiful women in the Windward Islands, was a sailor's dream town as it had been since the heyday of the pirate Henry Morgan.

Presently the guard brought Auguste his breakfast. It might be Fiesta upstairs, but here it was the same Spartan fare as always – bananas, a half loaf of bread, cold coffee and a jug of water. The tasteless breakfast alone was enough to make Auguste regret picking the pocket that led to his 60 day sentence. Consequently, when the guard paused to pass the time, Auguste was curt. So the guard finally shrugged his shoulders and left the prisoner alone with a day old newspaper to read to wile away his time.

Auguste looked at Wednesday night's St. Pierre paper "Les Colonies" 7 May 1902. An item on page one read, 'Thursday being the Feast of the Ascension, our offices will be closed tomorrow, our next number will not appear until Friday." There was to be no paper and no Friday for St. Pierre.

The harbor was not good, but it was the busiest in the West Indies. Actually, there was no true harbor, merely a roadstead shelving off so steeply that large ships could anchor within 100 yards of the shore. Colorful markets, shops and trading houses extended along the two-mile waterfront, and barefooted minstrels sang in the palm-shaded streets. Handsome "yellow" native women were dressed in brightly colored low-cut blouses with long sleeves, long skirts, turban-like head scarves, immense earrings and necklaces of hollow gold beads. They carried hundred pound stalks of bananas and bundles of laundry on their heads (no hands) as they walked up and down the narrow streets between the clean, pastel-colored stone houses and villas, each with its small garden of vivid red, yellow and purple flowers.

Only the night before this ultimate in disasters, the mountain had seemed friendly and put on a fascinating fireworks display which was almost hypnotic in its magnificence. Beginning like a Roman candle with fiery globes of flame, "Old Baldy" followed with sparklers and finally rained incandescent ashes like a whole box of multi-colored skyrockets with star clusters bursting over land and sea. The entire display was silhouetted against a black wall, backlit red.

Familiarity breeds contempt of the greatest dangers until they are thought no dangers at all. In 1792 the volcano had stirred in its slumber, but only to belch up a cloud of powdery gray ash which dusted lightly fertilizing the lush tropical vegetation for a few miles around. No one was killed, injured or even seriously inconvenienced. Mt. Pelee erupted again mildly in 1851, but only a few old timers remembered. Since then the mountain had smoked occasionally, but that was just a pleasant part of the scenery.

**The final addition of the St. Pierre paper read by the only survivor
of the town in his underground cell.**

Early in April, 1902, the smoke grew a bit more dense and dark and steam was seen issuing from a valley on the shoulder. A bunch of adventurers went up to take a look and found an old lake bed filled with water. They reported underground rumblings. On April 30th there were earth tremblings and muffled explosions. These were traditional volcanic warnings of impending danger, but the inhabitants of St. Pierre were more curious than afraid. Old timers began to talk again of 1851, and youngsters hoped for some new phenomena to silence all the old braggarts who prefaced each story with, "Now son, it was before your time, but I remember in '51 when..." Interest was running so high that the leading local newspaper advertised an excursion to the summit on May 4, "if the weather be fine."

But the weather was less than fine. Actually, the citizens were successfully (and tragically) mesmerized by the politically-directed stories in the local paper and posters displayed around town. In their efforts to contain the vote-casting populace through May 1, Election Day, they virtually ignored Pelee's ominous warnings by promoting one festive occasion after the next. Gray-white powder up to several inches blanketed the rural areas close to the volcano and dust-deadened branches littered the access roads for the excursion to the summit, which was canceled.

On May 2, there was a violent eruption with loud explosions and heavy clouds of condensed steam. Only the animals seemed instinctively to sense disaster and began leaving the slopes around the crater.

On May 4th at the Usine Guerin, a large sugar mill just north of the city there was a nightmarish invasion by ants and centipedes – countless thousands of small, yellowish speckled ants and horrid foot-long black centipedes, both species venomous enough in these numbers, to kill an adult. Driven from the slopes of Pelee by ash fall and tremors, they swarmed into the mill because it lay in the pathway of their retreat.

Many mill workers were badly bitten, as were their terrified animals, but none died. Less fortunate were the residents of another district of St. Pierre. Almost as if St. Patrick were in alliance with old Pelee, scores of snakes suddenly appeared in the streets. Included were the deadly fer-de-lances, pit vipers six feet or more in length whose bite is fatal within minutes. They swarmed the area, killing chickens, pigs, horses, dogs and slow men, women and children. Despite the marksmanship of soldiers firing through the streets for more than an hour to dispatch at least 100 fer-de-lances, some 50 humans and more than 200 animals died from their bites.

Swarms of migrating birds detoured their usual stop in the region, and those foolish enough to fly near the brewing holocaust dropped dead from noxious gas.

Soon the streets and garden were white with ash and alarmed sailors noted peculiar ground swells in calm seas and warm spots in the ocean. Notwithstanding rum and women, the U.S. sailors began thinking of leaving. Tropic thunder showers broke out repeatedly from disturbances in the atmosphere around the mountain.

Nothing further disastrous to human life occurred, however, until the 5th, when a side of the new lake was blown out and its water, rushing down the mountain, carried away trees and rocks in a river of mud which destroyed the already-tormented sugar mill,

Usine Guerin, and 30 persons in it, and finally plunging into the sea with such momentum that it raised a "tidal" wave (actually a seismic sea wave having nothing to do with tides) sinking two yachts and flooding the lower streets.

Most of this went on some distance from the city, but refugees brought their tales of natural horror in a world assailed by internal fires. After a time of curious disregard for danger, the people began to come down with a good case of the nerves.

Campaign conscious and preoccupied with the notion that the voters must not leave town before Election Day, they sent an urgent wire to the Governor of Martinique, Louis Mouttet at Fort de France, and he arrived to give reassurance to the poor and logical who knew he would not be there if there were danger. He admonished them to keep their heads, which is precisely what they wanted to do. A committee was appointed to study the matter, and posters were printed promising safety. Pelee protested with increasing thunder, but almost everybody believed the campaign promises of their politicians. The Governor even brought his wife to show he planned to stay. And just to make sure they had company, he reinforced the people's will power by stationing soldiers around the town to prevent any mass exodus.

For three days the volcanic horrors grew until terrified people spent their days and nights indoors. Many people would have tried to leave town in spite of the soldiers, but it seemed more secure inside their houses with friends than exposed even temporarily to the ash and soot raining down from Pelee's defective boiler. It exploded again and again with increasing fury. Tension and anxiety were built up by the volcano's warnings.

On May 7, there was a lull. The air cleared somewhat and "Old Baldy" put on a fireworks display for the public to see, at what seemed like a safe distance. The U.S. sailors set sail, the crowd saw them off and went home to their beds for a good night's sleep, more relaxed than they had been for days. The worst was over, they thought. Actually, the volcano was gathering strength for a blast no one could anticipate, since no explosion like it had ever occurred anywhere before.

Next morning brought earthquakes which shook people out of their houses and sent them down to the sea where the snakes, lizards, centipedes and ants had gone instinctively many days before.

The contents of Pelee's gas-bloated stomach were beginning to convulse. New flames shot out of the volcano's raw throat, deafening everyone's ear drums with a roar like the last sound before unconsciousness.

A blast of highly-heated gasses, heavier than air, mingled with white hot sand and shot out of the crater as a billowing, pink cloud which burst when it hit the outside air and headed down the mountain toward St. Pierre as a hurricane of fire, killing and blasting everything it touched with its super-heated breath.

A helpless mob pushed and mauled each other on the docks. With the sea at their backs, they saw this avalanche of flame coming toward them. In three seconds it reached the city, and in three more, the panic was over as a mass of humanity was hurled lifeless into the sea.

The Pearl of the Antilles discovered by Columbus destroyed by Mt. Pelee on May 8, 1902.

The last day – May 7th – Mt. Pelee smokes in the background.

To Captain Freeman, of the British steamship Roddam, an eyewitness, the eruption was a glimpse of hell that held his sailors spellbound while it raced toward them with its scalding kiss of death. Even the sea seemed to recede in horror from the withering blast as it was sucked back 300 feet into a whirlpool filling some new ocean bottom abyss. A flood of volcanic debris rushed in pursuit of the fleeing waters with the speed of an express train. Then a tidal wave swept again toward shore over the boiling debris, first lifting, then capsizing and splintering all but one of the 17 burning hulks that had been ships in the harbor. The one ship not swallowed in the boiling sea had its masts seared off as by an acetylene torch, and was manned by a dying crew. In what had been warehouses, thousands of rum casks exploded simultaneously in a stinking hot punch, which ran in blazing rivers down blackened streets to spread out on the sea in flames.

Captain Freeman's *Roddam* was far out in the roadstead with steam up when the hurricane of fire hit the water, driving ahead of it a solid mass of humanity. The ship frantically slipped her cable to back off and escape from hell through 50 miles of continuously raining hot ash and rock. Twelve of her officers and men were dead and all the others were severely burned.

Within hours after Pelee's initial harvest of death, the French cruiser *Suchet* landed at St. Pierre's to look for survivors. Others followed. Everywhere were bodies, bloating on the water or buried under walls toppled on the victims by the force of the blast. Relief crews found bodies whose skulls and abdomens were burst by the heat while others were killed by a destructive force and heat which passed so suddenly it did not have time to burn the clothes off the victims. One man's head was found thrust into a basin from which the heat had sucked up all the water.

The city looked as if it had been dipped into a white hot furnace and then set out to cool.

Animal bodies, full of moisture, glowed for a while and then became black, charred wrecks as did everything combustible. There was no identifiable wreckage as one type of ex-building was not recognizable from another. Bodies lay on the ground amidst heaps of hot mud, gleaming ashes and piles of volcanic stones.

Relief crews stacked corpses in piles and burned them as Pelee paid sullen respect with continuous salutes from her volcanic cannon. Looting began almost as soon as relief. In spite of continued eruption and horrible surroundings, ghouls began to land in small boats and rob the bodies of jewelry, rings and coins. Meanwhile, rescue missions cared for survivors in the outlying villages around St. Pierre and behind ridges which had partially shielded them from the avalanche of fire. There is ample opportunity in the chaos after a catastrophe for both good and bad in human nature to reassert itself. St. Pierre was no exception.

Many volcanoes have erupted with more total force and cubic output than Pelee, but none with so much friction and electricity. The mountain relieved itself with such velocity on two occasions (May 8 and 20) that dust particles collided in the upward blast and produced electro-magnetic waves so powerful that magnetic needles 5,500 miles away were put out of commission for many hours. Such disturbances were reported by observatories in Maryland, Kansas and Hawaii. (All of this has a great bearing or at least an analogy for the strange goings on in the Bermuda Triangle, beside which Pelee and La Soufriere have erupted.)

Ordinary tragedy comes in threes, according to superstition, but volcanic disasters seem to travel in pairs. Mt. Pelee, the volcanic A-bomb, is usually coupled with La Soufriere (The Sulfur Pit) 90 miles away on the island of St. Vincent. La Soufriere destroyed Georgetown one day before Pelee's St. Pierre passed into eternity.

La Soufriere is an old and re-occurring menace to the beautiful British island it created and periodically threatens to destroy. Daniel Defoe wrote of a major eruption in 1718 and in 1812 the volcano acted as a single escape valve for the entire Caribbean area.

In 1812, 35 days after a Caracas, Venezuela earthquake crushed 10,000 people in one minute, "underground cannon" frightened farmers in an area of 4,000 square leagues and troops were alerted for attack. These thunderous noises ended a few minutes later when Soufriere burst forth in one of history's greatest eruptions. Two years of earthquakes throughout Central America came to a sudden stop – but the process of relieving this subterranean pressure was so violent that beautiful St. Vincent Island (now a republic) was almost blown out of the sea.

The 1812 eruption is historically important for still another reason. It practically exterminated the last of the Carib Indians after whom the Caribbean Sea is named. The fierce Caribs were discovered on St. Vincent by Columbus. They fought enslavement by the Spanish, French and English with heavy losses but remained untamed to the end. Finally they were wiped out by their fire god – as they expected in accordance with a long-standing tribal prophecy.

The day after the wall of fire exploded through the city blasting everything in its path to oblivion.

**When Soufriere blows on St. Vincent, it makes the USA's war on Grenada
just south a pop gun by comparison.**

Because of the reminders of 1812, plus no election to divert official interest,
warnings were heeded when Soufriere began to heat up again in the spring of 1902. Most
of the north end of St. Vincent already was evacuated when the old fire mountain

"rocked with agony" and then spilled six main streams of lava over the lip of its crater to smother Georgetown, the island capitol. Fortunately, only 1,350 people were burned to death, most of these struck by lightning in weird volcanic storms. The entire island, 17 miles long and 10 miles wide, was devastated by the first thunderous blast which hypnotized both man and beast with fear. Like Pelee, the volcano continued erupting for many weeks. It provided a pyrotechnic spectacle for excursion boats from Grenada, Barbados and Santa Lucia, where curious natives wanted a chance to see one of the blazing volcanoes which had buried their homes and blighted their fields in gray-white ash.

The final results of these two long-term eruptions and accompanying earthquakes were not limited to the surface of land or sea. The bottom of the Caribbean was drastically altered as far away as Jamaica and Puerto Rico. Vessels ran aground in areas once more fathoms deep. The entire windward island area had to be resounded and rechartered.

All For St. Pierre But Not All For Pelee...
Or Her Ally, La Soufriere

The zone of cremation – the absolute destruction the whole city of St. Pierre was eight square miles, but Mt. Pelee was not satisfied with the annihilation of St. Pierre. After a second blast May 20th, as powerful as the first, the volcano settled down to a seven month bombardment which kept Martinique in a state of constant siege. In addition to the avalanches of fire on May 8th and 20th, there were other major eruptions on May 26, June 6, July 9 and August 21. Stinking gasses, burning sand, hot stones, mud rain, penetrating dust, ominous sounds and total darkness intermittently settled on the once beautiful island of Martinique bathing everybody still alive in ash, famine and pestilence. Others suffered flash burns or were struck by lightning. A St. Elmo's fire danced on every mast or protrusion daring to stick its head up into the sky. Some even died from pure fright. Hundreds spent their last days in the hills cut off from sea escape by encircling hot mud flows. Pelee combined the World War I horror of poison gas with the World War II blast of atomic energy, yet it preceded both and had more total explosive energy than both World Wars plus all other wars before and after.

In 200 days of activity, the mountain threw out a cubic mass of material one-fourth the size of the entire island of Martinique. At its highest velocity, it was discharging every minute one and one half the yearly output of the Mississippi in mud (40,000,000 cubic feet).

But the emphasis was on speed. Pelee's discharge was "jet propelled", sending a huge lick of flaming sand two feet thick and a quarter-mile wide five miles from the mountain to the sea in less than three minutes. The total incineration of St. Pierre took less than six seconds.

The Aftermath

Witnesses to St. Pierre came forward with tales of horror – and of incredible good fortune. On that fateful morning of May 8th, one of the island's most prominent planters, Fernand Clerc, was in his St. Pierre home with his family plus several friends. An early riser, he was preparing for breakfast when he happened to notice strange behavior of the barometer. The pointer was fluttering and swinging wildly. Seized by a premonition, Clerc immediately ordered his carriages made ready, but succeeded only in convincing his wife and four children to leave with him. His friends thought him over timid and stayed for breakfast – and to die.

Passing the American consul, Thomas Prentiss, and his wife on the consulate balcony, Clerc saluted and likewise called to them to accompany him, but they, too, declined.

A 45 minute climb into the hills brought Clerc and his family to one of his country houses three miles above and away from the city. At that point, Pelee erupted before their horrified eyes. Pelee's now familiar cloud seemed to topple over with a loud noise and tumble downward not up like most eruptions onto St. Pierre like a black fog.

Soon sunlight was blocked by the volcanic clouds and hot ash rained upon Clerc's hillside estate, rendering invisible his family standing just a few feet away. After 20 minutes of the hot, suffocating blackness, a strong wind began to plow the ashes away, revealing the devastation below. "Tongue or pen can never describe what I saw," Clerc said. "About me everywhere were my relatives and friends burning. I saw I could do no good – all were dead – not one alive. I hastened back and at first opportunity and sent my family, these that had escaped with me, to Guadalupe."

One of the most astonishing escapes was that of a young girl, Harviva Da Ifrile. On her way to church in St. Pierre, Harviva instead was sent by her mother on an errand to her aunt, who had a pastry shop halfway up the mountain. The shop was near an ancient crater, "Corkscrew", so named for the tourist trail which wound down to its floor where hungry tourists bought Harviva's aunt's pastries.

Approaching the Corkscrew, Harviva felt hot wind and saw tendrils of smoke coming from the pit. Three tourists were down in the pit trying to outrun a rising "boiling stuff" – which covered three bodies as it continued to the top of the Corkscrew. No longer curious, Harviva fled screaming down the road to St. Pierre. Just as she reached the road she looked back to see "the boiling stuff burst from the top of the Corkscrew and run down the side of the hill. It followed the road first, but then as the stream got bigger, it ate up the houses on both sides of the road. "Then I saw that a boiling red river was coming from another part of the hill and cutting off the escape of the people who were running from the houses," she said later.

Harviva ran to the shore and jumped into her brother's boat, rigged with sail. Behind her, as she readied to cast off the stone wharf, she saw her brother racing down the hill towards her. But he did not win the race.

Heading for a favorite grotto where she and her chums often played, she looked back to see the mountain open up and boil down on the screaming people. Though burned considerably by falling ash and rock, Harviva make it to the grotto. From the safety of her cave, she then heard an awful hiss as the boiling stuff hit the sea, filling the cave almost to the top with steaming water and rendering Harviva unconscious. She remembered nothing more until she was rescued two miles at sea by the French cruiser *Suchet*, who found her drifting in her broken and charred boat.

As news of Martinique's disaster was telegraphed around the world, relief was quick in coming. On behalf of the American people, President Roosevelt immediately gave $200,000. Lest that be considered a small sum, remember the value of money in those days; besides, the Kings of England and Italy each contributed only $5,000.

Additionally, Teddy Roosevelt ordered a fast and well-provisioned warship, *Dixie*, sent to aid Martinique, along with several scientists, who were assigned hammocks in *Dixie's* cramped quarters, as the first court to study what had happened in St. Pierre.

Among them were Edmund Hovey of the American Museum of Natural History and Thomas Jaggar Jr. of Harvard University, a brilliant geologist who henceforth devoted his life to the study of volcanoes. Joining these men in Martinique were other noted scientists and journalists from the United States and Europe, including Alfred Lacroix from the French Academy of Sciences. The catastrophe which destroyed St. Pierre gave such stimulus to the science of volcanology that 1902 became a landmark date in the history of man's effort to graph the workings of his planet.

Sifting through the wreckage, examining the evidence, and soon even witnessing further eruptions of Pelee, these "fathers of modern volcanology" evaluated, reported and theorized such as had ever before been done.

Eyewitness reports notwithstanding, apparently there had been no molten lava flow from Pelee at any time during the eruption. Instead, death and destruction were issued from a volcanic cloud formed of superheated steam and other gases made heavy by billions of particles of incandescent ash and traveling with enough force to carry along boulders and block of volcanic material.

As happens with scientific detective work, it took the chain reaction of over-lapping and contradictory theories of several of these talented men to lead to the final report of Lacroix, in mid-March of 1903. Lacroix's classic in the annals of volcanology entitled *The Pelean Type of Volcanic Eruption* describes the mass of incandescent lava (already blown to bits by the expansion of the gases it contains) which rises and rolls over the lip of the crater in the form of an avalanche of red hot dust. The horizontal nature of Pelee's blast was due to explosions from the side of the dome rising in the crater. This horizontal component, known as base surge, occurs in many Pelean type volcanic eruptions. The eruption demonstrated how the heavy gases can roll down hill in its destruction. The reason why came two months later in Mt. Pelee's erection.

The Volcanic Erection

Just in case you think there is nothing new with volcanoes – There was another fantastic aspect of the Martinique eruption in 1902 which has been seen in no other volcanic disturbance before or since. It was called the spine of Pelee, a tremendous tower that rose up 1,020 feet out of the crater and remained 5,020 feet above sea level as a single block of varicolored volcanic rock 350 to 500 feet thick at its base. In August, 1902, it began to rise like the Empire State Building on a slow freight elevator, often as much as 50 feet a day. It descended a year later never to rise again. In his book, *The Tower of Pelee*, Angelo Heilprin calls this volcanic phenomenon an "extraordinary obelisk of lava like a veritable Tower or Babel"… with… "steam and ash puffs and blue sulfur fuels playing about its base." Pelee's spine, according to Heilprin, "was merely the ancient core of the volcano that had been forced from its position of rest in which (lava) solidification had left it…" The power to lift, or even sustain, so gigantic a structure as this tower, with a cubical content equal to that of the Great Pyramid of Egypt, is so enormous it defies man's imagination, especially two months after the initial eruption and continuous eruptions thereafter had been using up the pressure Pelee had built up. Pelee's giant erection had to be stranger than any science fiction.

St. Pierre was a small village of 1000 inhabitants when the volcano erupted again in 1929. There was no difficulty getting the population to leave town. There is a large volcanologic museum to remind them of 1902, and evacuation drills are always well attended.

Looming like a monument to the 30,000 dead, the tower of Pelee jutted over 1000 feet above the summit. Created by unique geological forces, the tower destroyed itself within a year and its fragments were scattered around the volcano's peak.

How Pelee Helped Win The Canal For Panama

News of Mt. Pelee's 1902 eruption competed with an issue of great national importance in the United States. The American public was preoccupied with the planned construction of a Central American canal connecting the Atlantic and Pacific oceans. Not only was the canal a major engineering challenge, capable of establishing the U.S. as a symbolic world power, but such a passage was vital to the emerging U.S. Navy and merchant marine by obviating the need to travel 8,000 miles around Cape Horn.

The question was – where to construct such a canal? Inspired by their recent engineering triumph of digging the Suez Canal, in the 1880's the French had tried again with a waterway through the Columbian territory of Panama. After a decade of work costing $287,000,000 plus the lives of 20,000 men, their project was abandoned.

Mindful of the French fiasco, American government commissions and prominent politicians favored a route through neighboring Nicaragua. So doggedly the Panama lobbyists fought on, backed by American railroad magnates in line for additional profits to their already-controlled Panama Railway and by shareholders in the ruined French canal company hopeful to recoup by sealing its Panamanian assets.

The May eruptions of Mt. Pelee and La Soufriere suddenly riveted attention on Nicaragua's own volcanic nature. Previous rails about Nicaragua's 12 volcanoes had met with no success as only one volcano was anywhere near the proposed canal, and it was dormant. Now rejuvenated lobbyists hammered away at the "terrible object lesson" of Pelee. Even Vulcan contributed in late May and the news reached Washington that a Nicaraguan volcano was indeed erupting.

The clincher happened three days before the U.S. Senate was scheduled to vote on the route. Philippe Bunau-Varilla, formerly chief engineer of the French canal company but switched to a prominent lobbyist for Panama, prepared an elegant effort. His previous observation, "Young nations like to put on their coats of arms that best characterizes their native soil. What have the Nicaraguans chosen? Volcanoes!" still ringing in the halls of the Senate, Philippe canvassed every stamp dealer in the Washington area for a particular, inexpensive stamp. He mailed that Nicaraguan postage stamp – featuring a smoking volcano – to every Senator.

Thusly swayed by such inspired propaganda, and the eruptions of La Soufriere and Pelee, the Senate approved the Panama Canal by eight votes. Once again, the politicians had reacted to a panic caused by volcanoes. As the author of this volcano book, my personal relationship to the Panama Canal is that my father, the environmentalist, was also the inventor of railroad artillery equipment including the device through which the huge cannon mounted on flat cars could be lowered through the car to fixed mounts on both ends of the railroad going alongside the canal. These huge guns with their big bang helped man's efforts to protect the canal and make like a volcano.

The Stamp That Rerouted the Panama Canal

The site of the Panama Canal was probably determined by a Nicaraguan postage stamp sent to members of the U.S. Congress by an obsessed Frenchman, the engineer Philippe Jean Bunau-Varilla.

The U.S. fully realized the need for a canal across the midsection of the Americas when the battleship *Oregon*, desperately needed for the Spanish-American War, took 68 days to reach the Caribbean from San Francisco. By 1899, a bill was pending in Congress to build such a ~~canal~~ but through Nicaragua, not Panama. This put Bunau-Varilla in a tizzy. He had worked on the French Panama Canal project until its failure in 1889, then devoted himself to selling the French rights to the U.S.

Then, a fateful event: In May 1902, Nicaragua's Momotombo volcano erupted. The tragedy provided a golden opportunity for Bunau-Varilla. He found Nicaraguan postage stamps illustrating a smoking Momotombo and sent them to Congress. The implicit question: Why not choose a country without volcanoes—Panama, for instance? And, in 1904, Congress so voted.

Looking into the crater Soufriere (St. Vincent) – one of the largest active craters anywhere. The author takes a look guided by Dr. Mollie DeLozier and her husband Dr. Hugh DeLozier, then students from the medical school on Grenada and St. Vincent. Soufriere erupts too often to surprise. Its end of the island remains sparsely populated and ready for quick evacuation. The enormous quantities of water periodically cascading from this huge crater, give a good idea of the prevailing scientific theory that all new water on this earth comes from volcanoes and probably all water, old or new, is of volcanic origin.

There is a new sub peak rising in the
bottom of what was once a huge
and very deep lake crater.

Soufriere is never completely quiet,
always at least smoking.

The Roraima burned, demasted and drifting off St. Pierre the morning of May 9, 1902.

Eyewitness Account of the Death of St. Pierre

There were none within the city limits of St. Pierre but an eye witness from one of the ships in the harbor who tells the full story of St. Pierre better than any. "Leslie's Popular Monthly" magazine in July, 1902 ran this exclusive account by its badly burnt chief officer, Ellery Scott describing the volcanic sinking of the Quebec liner Roraima:

"Mine was one of the two ships not completely destroyed or swallowed in the boiling sea, although it was a miracle we escaped manned by a dying crew. Everything on the deck was burned as even our masts were seared off. I still dream of the horrors of that awful day when all of St. Pierre was hurled into eternity and turned into one big charnel house. But I must go back and tell you what we were doing there in the first place. 'We left New York on Saturday, April 26, 1902, aboard the Quebec Line Steamship Roraima, Captain Muggah, bound for Demerara, British Guiana, via stops in the Windward Islands. Our crew numbered forty-seven, and we had aboard twenty-one passengers – men, women and children. Through May 7th the trip was uneventful.'"

"That night as we lay at anchor off Dominica, I sat out on the deck in the cool breeze and amused myself thinking of St. Pierre's rum distilleries and of how its French-speaking beauties loved a good time. St. Pierre was a good liberty town in any sailor's little black book, and had been a favorite port call since Henry Morgan and his pirates held sway there."

"At 1:00 a.m. when we hove anchor and made a course south by east-half-east for Martinique, none of us realized we were to witness the last day of St. Pierre, or that most of us would die there before another sunset."

"Everything went well until 4:45 a.m. I was on the bridge for the morning watch. The night was fair and the sea calm. Suddenly without warning we came into thick, heavy smoke and falling ash off the northeast end of the island of Martinique. This disturbed me so much that I called the captain and asked what he thought of the weather. I had never seen an active eruption in the islands before, but years ago I had seen Etna aflame, so I knew something about volcanoes; and of course we had every reason to suppose that the smoke was from Mt. Pelee. The wind at this time was to the east of south, and the smoke blew directly toward us."

"We skirted the island, keeping about two miles off-shore, but on account of the currents that were setting us in toward the land, we had to steer various courses, sometimes hauling off and at other times drawing in. The current was never steady, but it ran very strongly, and we took for granted that this was due to some volcanic action going on. To a certain extent the captain and I were alarmed. It was a fine dust, a sharp gray ash, which was falling."

"At 6:15 a.m. we anchored off St. Pierre. Just before that, as we were making the harbor, we passed the site of a sugar refinery which had stood at the mouth of the bay. There was but a single smokestack left to mark the spot.

"We anchored inside of the outer buoys, using the starboard anchor and the forty-five fathom shackle, according to the pilot's instructions, just outside the line of shipping lying there and some seven hundred yards offshore. We did not make fast to the buoys, so that we might get away quickly if necessary."

"A peddler rowed out to us with a boatload of doves and starlings which he offered for sale. I asked him where he got so many, and he pointed to the volcano. It seems a large flock of birds flew too close to the crater and were poisoned by the fumes. Thousands of them fell dead in and around the crater and were gathered up by the basketful to be sold for choice squabs. We didn't buy any."

"The harbor master and doctor soon came alongside and passed the ship. The next to come aboard were our company's agents, Messrs. Plessoneau and Testarte. The captain had a talk with them and asked whether they thought there was any danger from the volcano. Dense columns of smoke were then rising majestically from the peak of Mt. Pelee and ascending towards heaven. But at this time it was perfectly clear over the harbor, for we were full five miles to the south of the mountain. The agents were very reassuring. They gave Captain Muggah a complete report."

"There had been no damage done since the destruction of the sugar refinery a few days before, said our agents, and the volcano was calming down. Plessoneau and Testarte both said, however, that a number of people wanted to get away to St. Lucia. The citizens, including Plessoneau's wife, were not so much afraid of the volcano now as of snakes. It seemed that the volcanic activity had caused a real reptile panic, with snakes and lizards leaving their homes in the cracked and craggy old lava fields around Pelee's crater to invade the city. St. Pierre was infested with snakes, including the dreaded fer-de-lance, whose bite was fatal. The city's streets and gardens described so beautifully in the guide book were now flour-white with ash, but so far the only deaths in St. Pierre itself were from snakebite."

"As we had a cargo for St. Lucia, the captain asked me to go through the holds and find whether it was possible to get at the cargo without unloading most of the goods for Martinique. I found we would have to move a great deal of Martinique cargo, so Captain Muggah decided that it was wisest for us to stop where we were and discharge the cargo. The reason that we had not got to work on it earlier that morning was that the 9th of May being Ascension Day, there were special services in all the churches of the city. Grand Mass was being said at the cathedral, and the rich people had come over to St. Pierre to attend it. Laborers and everyone else were religiously inclined for that day, and it would have been difficult in any case to secure stevedores promptly, for, since the first eruption of Mt. Pelee, business at St. Pierre had been suspended to a great degree. In fact, the stores had been open for only one solitary half-hour the day before, and the people of the banks, as a precautionary measure, had transferred their books and other valuables to a French man-of-war which was lying off Fort de France. It was evidently impossible for us to discharge any cargo that day. We must wait until next morning. This, however, did not stop several passengers taken on board at the other islands and bound for Martinique from going ashore."

"Meantime, our sailors, under the boatswain, were cleaning up the ashes and dust which lay fully a quarter-inch thick over everything – just like white sand. The ship was covered with it from end to end. It had sifted into everything. When the captain and I came off the bridge, our uniforms were completely covered with it. Passengers and crew were gathering up the sand and ashes to keep as mementos. Some would put it in envelopes, others in tin tobacco boxes, and I can remember a big Negro giving me a cigar box filled with it, which I took, little thinking what a great plenty of it I should have before I ever made home again."

"Meantime the officers were grouped forward on the deck enjoying the grand view of Pelee as huge volumes of smoke rise from it. The smoke appeared to roll right up into the heavens, and then southward and easterly winds drove it away to the sea, so that where we were lying the air was comparatively clear. The sun was shining brightly, and everything appeared to be favorable except the column of black smoke."

"It was a few moments past eight in the morning by the ship's time. As we stood talking, the third engineer said to me, 'I must get my camera. I have only one more plate, but this is a sight that must not be missed.' With this he turned and made for his cabin. I never saw him again. Just then, all at once there was a sublime outburst from the mountain. Whether more than one crater opened, it would be difficult to say, but a conflagration came right out of the mountain in one grand burst, with a noise so terrible that beside it a thunderclap would sound like a pistol shot beside the roar of a twelve-inch gun. Then it came rolling down the mountain over the intervening hills – the molten slag, flame and smoke, one immense cloud of it – luminous, awful, rolling down like fire. It took just a moment. As it came sweeping down, there seemed to be an inexhaustible supply following it, an endless tornado of steam and ashes and burning gas. The instant we saw this grand outbreak coming toward us, the captain rushed to the bridge calling to me to heave up anchor. I sprang forward to the steam windlass. The carpenter beside me was bending forward to start the machine when destruction struck us."

"The thing was indescribable. It seemed to whirl earth and sea before it, just as the western cyclones wipe up the trees and everything in their paths! But this was an explosive whirlwind, setting fire to everything as it went. It was only a few seconds of time, but as it rolled over the intervening miles toward the city, that city was doomed.

Fire, ashes, smoke – everything combined – swept down on us in an instant. No railroad train could have escaped it."

"We could see only one side of the torrent, but more of it was pouring down the rear of the mountain, creating a tremendous backdraft and increasing the fury about us still further. Then came darkness blacker than night, and as the awful rain struck the waters, it just rolled along, setting fire to the shore and the ships. The Roraima rolled and careened far to port, then with a sudden jerk she went to starboard, plunging her lee rail far under water. The masts, smokestack, rigging – all were swept clean and went by the board. The iron smokestack came off short, and the two steel masts broke off two feet above the deck, perfectly clean, without a jagged edge, just like a clay pipestem struck with a big stick. We had started to heave the anchor, but it never left the mud. There we were, stuck fast in hell."

"The darkness was something appalling. It enveloped everything, and was broken only by the burning clouds of consuming gas which gave bursts of light out of the darkness. The ship took fire in several places simultaneously, and men, women and children were dead in a few seconds of time. This was a few minutes after eight o'clock."

"The saloon and the after end of the ship blazed up at once. The Roraima was lying with a heavy list to starboard, pointing toward the shore. Hot ashes fell thickly at first. They were soon followed by a rain of small hot stones ranging all the way from the size of shot to pigeon's eggs. These would drop in the water with a hissing sound, but where they struck the ship's deck they did little damage, for the decks were protected with a thick coating of ashes from the first outburst. After the stones came a rain of hot mud, lava ash apparently mixed with water, of the consistency of very thin cement. Wherever it fell, it formed a coating clinging like glue, so that those who wore no caps it coated, making a complete cement mask entirely over their heads."

"For myself, when I saw the storm coming, I snatched a tarpaulin cover off one of the ventilators and jammed it down over my head and neck, looking out through the opening. This saved me much, but even so, my beard, face, nostrils and eyes were so filled with the stuff that every few seconds I had to break it out of my eyes in order to see. This mud was not actually burning, but it steamed, and there was heat enough in it to dry on the head and form a crust so that it fitted like a plaster cast. I remember that Charles Thompson, the assistant purser, a fine-looking burly black from St. Kitts, who stood beside me, had his head so weighted down with the stuff that he seemed to feel giddy and was almost falling. When he asked me to break the casing off his head, I was afraid it would scalp him. I could feel the heat on my own head very plainly through my tarpaulin cover, and his scalp must have been badly scorched."

"All persons were not on deck at this time. Some of the passengers were dressing, some still in their bunks. In some cases they were poisoned almost instantaneously by the noxious gas. In others they were drowned by the water which swept in through the open portholes of the submerged staterooms on the starboard side."

"The darkness was appalling, lit only by the flames from the after end of the ship and the lurid glare of the conflagration on shore when a large warehouse caught fire, and the great puncheons of rum burst with a loud report and shot their blazing contents into the air. At this time I went to the lower bridge, feeling my way along in order to find the captain. On the bridge I almost stumbled upon a crouching figure with a hideous face burned virtually beyond recognition. 'Who are you?', I cried, for I did not recognize him in the darkness. The man looked up, his face terrible to see. 'Mr. Scott,' he said, 'don't you know me?' I said, 'My God, it's the captain!' He got on his feet as best he could then, and seeing one of the boats still hanging in a crippled condition, he wanted to know if we couldn't clear her away."

"Well, Captain,' I said, 'the boat is stove in and of no use, and she is jammed so that twenty men couldn't budge her, and we have no one to help us.'"

"Just then Benson, the carpenter, and Thompson, the assistant purser, came on the bridge. Thompson was horribly scorched, while Benson's principal burns seemed to be on his hands. The captain ordered the boat cleared away anyhow. With a knife I cut the forward davit tackle fall, but she wouldn't move. She was jammed. It was impossible to get her clear, and when he found that it was impossible, the captain said, 'Mr. Scott, jump overboard and save yourself.'"

"No, Captain,' said I, 'I won't leave the ship.'"

"Well,' said he, 'find out how the ship is and what is the condition of our people. Find out how the women and children are.'"

"After looking about and finding the after end of the ship all on fire and people burned and dying everywhere, and flames breaking out in several places forward, I went back to report to the captain. When I reached the bridge, he was gone. He had either fallen or jumped overboard to relieve his own suffering, which must have been very terrible."

"There were only four of us really able-bodied – Benson, the carpenter, Thompson, the assistant purser, a black laborer from St. Kiss, and I. The men who helped us were horribly burned, but it was wonderful to see their heroism. Two engineers who had all but lost the flesh on their hands were still carrying things about to help us, using their upper arms and elbows. The command devolved upon me."

"The first thing to be done was to get the fires extinguished forward (for the wind was blowing offshore and raking the ship) so that we should not be cremated alive. Fortunately the water was calm. It appeared as though the thick rain of mud had smoothed the water, but it still swirled and rolled past us, owing to the volcanic currents. The pumps had no steam and wouldn't work, but every man still able to walk did his best. Two of them began to lower buckets over the side and then, forming a fire line, we passed them up forward and dashed the water at the flames."

"All this time, thick darkness continued. Then all at once about nine o'clock it lightened a little, and we could see the steamer Roddam steaming straight toward us as though coming to take us off. We had no means of knowing that she was almost as badly off as we were, for she had steerageway and came up close enough for us to see that the forward part of her was all right. We took for granted that she had been out of the line of fire. This looked like a rescue, and we thanked God. Some of us got the passengers, women and children, on the upper deck forward, hoping that the Roddam would come near enough to take them aboard."

"Suddenly, not more than a hundred feet away, she stopped. We said, 'Well, perhaps she doesn't see us.' I ran at once to the shell house and grabbed a handful of signal lights. Two of them I found were blue lights and one the company's special signal. We set them off (they burned brightly, like fireworks), trying to attract the Roddam's attention and to show her that some living people were aboard, but to our horror the ship slowly backed out into the darkness, leaving us absolutely disheartened. When the others spoke about it to me, I said, 'She has only backed out of the line of smoke. She will come back again and take us off', but after a while the wind veered south, the smoke cleared, and we could see nothing more of her."

"This was about 8:45 a.m. How long we could stay afloat was the question. There was no time for deliberation. All of us who could rushed to the life belts, which were distributed throughout the ship among every living soul aboard. When a mother had a child in her arms, we would pass the preserver around both of them."

"The next thing was to find out what condition our battered hull was in, and to put out the small fires which had ignited again here and there. The worst one was in the port steerage, far forward. The steerage quarters, as it had happened, had been freshly cleaned and painted at Demararaa, the mattresses were neatly piled inside, while the door was kept locked lest the crew should steal the beds. The starboard ports, however, were left open and the volcanic fire sweeping in ignited the mattresses. We tried to open the door, but finding it fast, several of us grasped a big plank and making a battering-ram of it, smashed the door. Two great piles of mattresses were afire. It was a bad outlook, for if the fire gained headway there, it would sweep the ship, and worse than this, we had a matter of three thousand cases of kerosene oil, great kegs of varnish and barrels of tar stowed away in the forward hold of the ship not a dozen feet from the fire."

"Out on the deck, just over the steerage quarters, were the cattle pens which were used to store some thousands of spruce timber, enough to burn a city, and standing about close by were a number of puncheons of temper lime, a highly inflammable substance used in the making of sugar. This temper lime, which takes fire if it comes in contact with water, was already smouldering and the smoke was hanging thickly about it."

"It was a bad fight, this at number one hatch. Two of us lowered buckets over the side and hauled up water, while the others dashed it upon the mattresses. The water would quiet the flames for a moment, and then one of us would rush in, pull out a mattress and throw it overboard. But the instant a smouldering mattress came into the current of air outside, it would blaze up again, and it needed lively work to get one clear without getting badly burned."

"All this was exhausting work, but there was more to follow. We soon saw that the firemen's quarters on the starboard bow were breaking out in flames. We fought them hard and steadily, and again dragged out the mattresses one by one, and more than once as we did so, out with the mattress would come the lifeless body of some messmate who had died, trapped like a rat."

"After a time all the smaller fires were under control and we got a breathing spell so that we could look about us. The sight was fearsome. All around us were sailors and passengers, men, women and children, burnt and dying, crying aloud for water."

"Thompson, the assistant purser, who was such a great help to me throughout the struggle, had an interesting story to tell afterward. He had seen the ruin coming, but had time to fling himself through the open doorway of his stateroom and close the door. The next instant the ship veered over and water hot from the fire sweeping over it poured into his cabin until he was submerged to his neck. Then the ship righted, the water receded and Thompson struggled out on the starboard alley and came upon two women horribly burned and begging piteously for water. He rushed into a neighboring stateroom which was half-filled with water, and finding a can was about to fill it from the little tank of fresh water above the basin, when he felt something soft beneath his foot. Looking down, he saw the dead face of a man."

"Then hurrying out to the officer's messroom he ran to the water tank. Within it the water was thick and muddy and almost hot. Fortunately there was still a big cake of ice in it, and this he dumped into his bucket and carried it out to the unfortunates to cool their mouths."

"Gradually we collected the survivors and laid them on deck forward near hatch number one, all of them crying for water, but many of the unfortunates could not drink at all. The flaming gases had burned their mouths and throats and even the linings of their stomachs so terribly that in many cases the passage of the throat was almost entirely closed, and many of the unhappy creatures could not swallow a drop. When we put the water into their mouths, it stayed there and almost choked them, and we had to turn them over to get the water out; still they would implore us for more. Fortunately, the darkness was beginning to lift now, the flaming city supplying us with plenty of light. We broke open the ice-house door and hauled out blocks of ice and broke them into small pieces. These the survivors could hold in their mouths when they could no longer drink. Several persons had their tongues burned out. The coatings of their mouths and tongues and the linings of their noses were some times entirely gone, so that when they attempted to draw breath, the air would block their throat and nostrils and smother them."

"All this time the groans and shrieks of the sufferers were heartbreaking. You read about that fellow down in hell looking up and asking for water? Well, that is about as near as I can come to describing it, but everything that happened stays in my mind like a nightmare. I can see now one of the passengers, a man lying on the foc's'le deck, hideously scarred, crying for water. When we gave it to him, he could not drink it. It would not pass down his throat. He was crawling around the deck on his hands and knees calling for water, and fearing that he would fall overboard, with the assistance of another man I brought him down to the main deck. As soon as he got there, he caught sight of Thompson with his water can, and at once began to crawl after him for water, like a dog. Thompson gave him the water, but he could not swallow, and the only way to keep him from following around after the water can was to attend to him and no one else, so the poor wretch had to be left. The man's tongue was literally burned out of his head. His arms were cruelly burned from his shoulders to his fingertips. As he lay there moaning aloud in mortal agony, one of the sailors happened to put a bucket of salt water near him. The man plunged his right arm into it to relieve the scalding pain. At once his skin broke straight round his shoulder and stripped from his arm until it hung like a lady's opera glove turned inside out from the tips of his fingers. But the worst burns were internal. The fire did not seem to penetrate clothing, but burned the exposed flesh mercilessly."

"I saw one little coffee-colored baby, fearfully scorched, lying in the arms of a nurse called Clara, who had come from New York with a family named Stokes. The child was dying, with its tongue lolling out of its mouth and the skin of the tongue all gone. There was still life in the little thing, and as Thompson came along, he gave the baby some water, but it was of no use. Clara's arms were badly burned, and at last she had to lay the child down. When she did so, the second engineer, Evans, picked the infant up with his scorched hands and held it gently until it died in his arms. Then he laid the infant in one of the deck staterooms. The door was open so that we could all see, and the sight was so pitiful that I went in, and shaking a pillow out of its case, put the little disfigured body inside and laid it on the bed so that it looked decent and Christian. I am thankful to say that Clara survived and went to the hospital. I think there is a good prospect of her recovery."

"The same Clara helped us take care of Mrs. Stokes and her three children, two boys and a girl. The wretched woman's mouth could not open and her teeth were set. We took a small spoon and put some crushed ice between her teeth, and could hear her murmur thanks. Poor creature, she did not live long enough to see two of her children die. The boy died ten or fifteen minutes later. We later transferred the baby (who was an infant in arms) and the eldest girl to the rescue boat, but the baby died before she reached land. These two children and a woman from Martinique were the only people who cared for anything to eat. Thompson found some food keeping warm in the oven of the storeroom. Every eatable thing outside had been destroyed."

"There was another woman, a Mrs. McAllister. Thompson, who was busy seeing after everyone, got a bed out of the men's quarters and set it down in the damp mud on deck so that she could rest there. She lay still for a while and then called Clara, the nurse girl. 'Won't you sing a couple of hymns for me?' she asked, 'and offer a short prayer, for I am dying.' The nurse knelt down in the ashes and began to sing –

'Rock of Ages, cleft for me,
Let me hide myself in Thee.'

We could hear only snatches of the hymn, for we had work to do, but in each lull we could hear her sweet voice. She sang again, 'Safe in the Arms of Jesus' and then, clasping her hands, looked up to heaven and offered a short prayer. Then Mrs. McAllister thanked her and bade her goodbye."

"By this time the air was getting a little purer, so that it was possible to breathe. The first fierce blast had been so strong and fiery that it struck men dead on the spot.

"While Thompson and Thomas, a laborer, were trying to alleviate the sufferings of the dying, Benson, the carpenter, and I went through the different holds of the ship. We found the hull tight. What water was in her had come down her hatches when she first keeled over. We sounded under the ship and found twenty-five fathoms of water, then the second engineer reported that the engines and boiler were safe and that there was no danger of an explosion. The second and fourth engineers were seared with fresh scars, but they stayed at their posts to see that the boilers were safe before they left them. It was out of the question to get up steam, however, for there was no smokestack and consequently no draught, and if there had been, there was no one to keep the fires going. Besides, even if the ship had been able to steam off before the wind, the flames in her stern would have swept her decks, instead of burning quietly at the after end of her as she lay at anchor."

"There was but one thing to do, so with the assistance of those who could do anything at all, we started to construct a raft. First of all, we lowered over the side two cargo skids fully eighteen feet long. These skids are placed in the wake of gangways to protect the ship's sides when the cargo is swung out by a derrick. The carpenter then let himself down, and after lashing the skids firmly together, I passed lumber down to him from the stock in the cattle pen, and this he spiked to the skids and made a raft secure and large enough to carry all who were living on board the ship. We counted the survivors and found we had twenty-four."

"All this took considerable time, and after we got the raft itself constructed, the next thing was to provision her. The Roraima carried four boats. Three had been destroyed and the fourth was jammed on the davits, but from her we got oars and rowlocks. We also passed down a compass, lanterns, cases of provisions, a can of oil and kegs of water. We got everything ready in case the fire from the after end of the ship should drive us out before some other means of relief came to us."

"It was between 2:00 and 3:00 p.m. that a French man-of-war, Suchette, Captain Pierre LeBris, steamed into the harbor of St. Pierre."

"We saw her coming toward us, but after our experience with the Roddam, I did not feel sure of anything. We got out the British ensign and tying it bottom upward on a stick, lashed it on one of the port davits, that being the highest stick left on the ship."

"The Suchette at once answered the signal and sent a boat alongside. We were the first ship she noticed. No other ship was showing any special signals to attract her attention, and all we could make out of the craft about us were merely burning hulks. Soon she sent two other boats to our aid, towed by a steam launch. Gradually we got the passengers over the side to the raft, from which they could be carried more safely to the boats. Those who were most helpless and maimed we lowered first, and those best able to help themselves were left until the last. After the passengers came the crew, then the officers. The second engineer went ahead, and I followed last."

"Just before I went over the side, I caught sight of a solitary sheep, the last of thirty which had been swept overboard. The poor creature was bleating pitifully, so I went back and laid open its head with an axe, which seemed to me a mercy. We left behind us between twenty and thirty dead bodies, some lying about the deck, some in the foc's'le, some in their bunks, where they had been smothered at the first fearful burst of poison gas. My own poor boy was there somewhere. From the moment of the explosion, I never saw him again. He was a likely young fellow, and used to say how some day he would have a ship of his own, and would take me along as mate, but I was determined that he should give up the sea and go to college and become a lawyer. This was to have been his last voyage. As we went away, some of the bodies looked so awful that we could not bear to look at them. The only thing I think of now is this – how did we ever come through it all and live to escape the madhouse?"

"At the time we left the ship, she was afire from her bulkhead. As we looked back, we saw a strange thing. A common reed chair, such as one often sees on the deck of a trans-Atlantic liner, was hanging in the air from the ship's stern. It had been fastened to the after flag and branched below so that it hung in space just beyond reach of the flames. Some poor devil had rigged it there and sat in it to save himself from the fire, afraid to jump on account of the fierce rush of the volcanic currents below. We had seen him there, sitting in his chair, long before we left the ship, at the back of the solid wall of fire which separated us from him, and he must have suffered terribly before he dropped from his perch and went overboard. We could not get to him because of the fire in the forward part of the saloon, but a stateroom was at hand with plenty of lifebuoys, and he might have got one and put it on; but strangely enough, after all that fire, there hung the empty chair literally intact. The next morning, the 9th, when the ship Corona steamed into the harbor of St. Pierre, the captain said that the chair still hung there unharmed."

"The Suchette then steamed slowly to Fort de France, her boats searching the shore and sea and picking up everyone found alive. Wreckage and driftage were scattered everywhere over the water, and now and then you could see a plank with an arm or leg curled over, while the remainder of the corpse was hidden beneath the surface.

At 9:00 p.m. she landed at the pier at Fort de France, where a quantity of stretchers were used to carry the wounded to the ambulances and thence to the hospitals. Clara, the nurse, and four of us men alone were able to walk those few steps.

"I said that the last I saw of Captain Muggah was on the bridge in the first hideous moments of darkness. Later, I heard more of him. It seems that just after I left him to work at the boats, Dan, the ship's cooper, a black laborer whom we had taken on at St. Kitts, saw him slip and fall overboard. The ship had a list and her deck was covered with slippery mud, so his fall was probably accidental. But whether he jumped or not, no man can say. If he did jump, in that mortal agony, who is there willing to blame him?"

"Well, Dan saw the captain go, and catching up one of the hatches, he leaped right after him, and striking out in the whirling current, put the hatch under the captain's arm to help support him in the water. Then he swam for shore, pushing his burden ahead of him, but there was such a tremendous current that he could make little headway, and gradually drifted alongside a burning hull which lay a few cable's length from the Roraima. Some of the crew who were frantic to escape hauled him toward them and then threw over a booby-hatch, which Dan made fast to his own raft. Then the men tossed down some bedding on which Dan laid the captain and one or two unfortunates from the other ship, who were lowered from the burning deck. Two or three sailors followed, and then all together they started the raft toward the shore, stopping every now and then to pick up some poor wretch floating in the water."

"As they were paddling painfully along, using pieces of board for oars, they sighted a small boat, which the natives of Martinique use, similar to a canoe with high sides. One of the sailors, a native, at once jumped overboard and swam to the boat. As soon as he climbed into her, he started back toward the raft, but on his way he came across another Martinique man clinging to a spar. He took him aboard and then, since two of them could paddle the boat with ease, he suddenly lost interest in his companies on the raft, and right there in plain sight of his messmates, turned and made off toward Fort de France."

"This was too much for the crew of the raft. They lost their nerve. Dan, the cooper, did his best to make them drive their raft back to the ship, but they absolutely refused to return and made for the shore. Eventually they reached land, but just as they struck the shore, Captain Muggah died. During all the hours on the raft he was more or less conscious, and in spite of his awful suffering he kept begging Dan not to go to the shore for safety, but to take him back to his ship. Try as he would, however, Dan could not induce the men to do this. No sooner had he landed than he got a stick of timber and started all alone to swim back to the ship. He reached the raft and brought me news of Captain Muggah's last hours, and also of their officer, Thompson, who had reached the shore alive."

"Twenty-eight survivors of the Roraima, four of them women, were taken aboard the Suchette. Not all of them reached Fort de France alive. Some died on the way, others were dead before the next morning; how many, I could not find out. On the morning of the 9th, when I tried to go to the hospitals, I could secure a permit to enter only one. There I came upon the second engineer and carpenter, the fourth engineer, the quartermaster and two sailors. Two had died during the night, one a fireman. Everything possible was being done for the poor fellows, but the doctor told me that the burns were all poisonous, and that wherever a scar was deep, blood poisoning was apt to set in."

"The next day I encountered a sailor from the Suchette, which went back to St. Pierre to look for more survivors after dropping us at Fort de France. He was one of the initial search crew and had been relieved when a burning wall fell and smashed his left arm. He said he didn't mind the mangled arm, that it was better than to stay in St. Pierre with the stink of burned human flesh and the horrors of hell all around him. Everywhere he went, he found bodies, floating on the water or buried under walls toppled by the force of the blast. The corpses were stacked in piles and burned. There were bodies whose skulls and abdomens were burst by the heat, while other victims were destroyed by flame which passed so suddenly it did not have time to burn off their clothes, yet it cauterized their insides with one white-hot breath."

"The next day, May 10th, our company's ship, the Corona, touched at Fort de France after trying to make a rescue at St. Pierre. I was deemed able to travel and they took be aboard along with a few others who were bandaged but not bedridden."

"We stopped at the British colony at St. Lucia for coal, and there I visited the Roddam, the only other ship which escaped from St. Pierre on May 8th. I found the ship in charge of a watchman and two policemen. She had been abandoned by all the survivors of her crew. When I went aboard, the watchmen was engaged in gathering up fragments of human bodies and putting them away in a locker. He discontinued the work to show me around."

"The Roddam presented an awful spectacle. She looked as if she had been thrust into soft, clinging mud and pulled out again. The mud stick and clung to her like cement, and was two feet deep on her decks. Awnings, stanchions and boat covers had been burned or swept away. Tarpaulins, rails, stays, hatch covers and even her smokestacks were gone. When the watchman dug into the lava, he found here and there fragments of human remains. About all that was left of the ship was her hull, and that, being of iron, had escaped destruction."

"Hearing that Captain Freeman was at the Hotel Felile, I called upon him. I wanted to get from his own lips the story of his escape and why he had not taken on survivors from the Roraima. I was unprepared for the terrible sight which greeted my eyes when I entered the room."

"Captain Freeman's face was burned to the color of teakwood, and large patches of skinned flesh were burned from his bones here and there. Both his hands were swathed in bandages. His hair and mustache were gone, his eyes were bandaged, and he was in great pain. When I told him who I was, he talked a great deal, to relieve himself, he said, of his suffering."

"He said the Roddam had been in St. Pierre only an hour when the eruption occurred. He was talking to an agent in the boat alongside when a big black squall approached the ship from the land. It was like a wall, traveled fast, and was accompanied by a tidal wave and a deafening roar. The sun disappeared immediately."

"Captain Freeman said that he shouted to everyone to stand clear. An instant later the air was filled with flame and batches of falling fire. The ship was immediately ablaze from end to end, and the crew laborers aboard began to rush about, frantic with pain. As nearly as he could remember, there were forty-two persons aboard the ship, only six of whom survived. The ship keeled over when the tidal wave hit, and nearly capsized. Then she righted and the falling shower of fire continued."

"Captain Freeman ran into the chart room, but was driven out again by flames that came in at the porthole. Then he rushed to the engine room telephone and signaled the engineer to put on full steam. Someone responded, and the ship began to move, but the steering gear was jammed and would not work. He kept the engines going ahead and astern alternately, hoping to free the paddles, and in so doing nearly collided with our ship, the Roraima, from which clouds of steam and flame were rising. He said he saw men on the Roraima wringing their hands and rushing about frantically, but could do nothing for us since his own ship was in such distress. He saw men from our ship jump into the sea, where they must have died instantly, for the water was boiling like a cauldron, a mass of boiling mud. Many of the Roddam's crew had disappeared, probably swept overboard, and the rest went one by one until only six were left. Every one of them must have died a terrible death."

"After a time the captain got the steering gear working, the ship answered her helm, and he headed her out to sea."

"During the run out of the harbor, the chief engineer died a horrible death. He escaped the first shock, started the engines, and not finding his men below, went on deck to look for them. As he thrust his head out the hatch, a hot blast hit him, burning one side of his face completely off."

"Slowly the sky cleared, and it was possible for Captain Freeman to see about him. Men in the red-hot debris lay crying all along the way. He himself, though he stayed at the wheel, was unable to lift his burned arms. Blood from his forehead kept running into his eyes, obscuring his vision. He likened his escape to the passage from hell into heaven. At last he reached the open sea, and with the help of two sailors, two engineers and the boatswain succeeded in taking his ship to St. Lucia."

"I did not have the heart to ask him why he did not stop his ship to help the Roraima. I would not have thought it possible before I saw it, but the Roddam was hit even harder than we were, and I'll never know how she escaped with anyone alive to tell of it."

"On May 11th, the day after I saw Captain Freeman and the Roddam at St. Lucia, I shipped on the Etonia with Captain Cantell to go home. The Etonia steamed back by the doomed city on its way to New York."

"The weather was clear and we had a fine view, but the hold outlines of St. Pierre were not recognizable. The formation of the land itself seemed to have changed. When we were about eight miles off the northern end of the island, Mount Pelee began to belch a second time. I had been watching the island from the time we first picked it up until we were well past St. Pierre, and I had just gone below, put up my glasses and stretched out on my bunk for a nap, when the captain sent for me. As I came on the bridge, he said, 'Look at that island, will you?'"

"I looked, and there the volcano was belching out a black cloud of what looked like dense smoke."

"Get below,' he said to the chief engineer, Farrish, 'and drive her as hard as she will stand until we get clear of this place. We don't want a repetition of the Roraima's experience, do we, Scott?' I agreed, and shuddered to think it might happen again."

"Clouds of smoke and lava shot into the air and spread over all the sea, darkening the sun. Our decks in a few minutes were covered with a substance that looked like sand dyed brown, and which smelled like phosphorus."

"I was standing the watch with Captain Cantell. When partial darkness came upon us, it is needless to say that I was badly frightened. I did not know but that we were to be buried under red-hot lava or engulfed by another tidal wave, though we were ten miles from shore."

"Crowd on steam!' I whistled down to the engineer, and he needed no urging. Slowly we drew away through a suffocating atmosphere, foot by foot, yard by yard, and at last the sun began shining again. We had passed outside the storm of dust and sand. When I looked at my watch, I found that we had been about an hour reaching daylight."

"Engineer Farrish gave her all the coal the furnaces could take. We had good coal and plenty of it, and we did not hesitate to use it. He pounded her through at an increase of two knots an hour over what the captain said he had always thought was the ship's highest speed. The safety valves were dancing a jig every minute, but, notwithstanding the high rate of speed at which we were running, there was scarcely a minute during the hour that we were flying from the scene of the eruption when the head of steam in the boilers did not force the safety valves open."

"When the engineer came on deck two hours later, we had left the island, hull down, but the decks of our ship were a sight. Everywhere everything was covered with the blue lava dust, which the force of the volcanic eruption had driven in the face of the wind ten miles out to sea and scattered over us."

"This dust as it fell on the ship was moist and sticky. It made the decks slippery, much as though they had been plastered with soft clay. When it dried out, it became like a fine powder. In many places the decks were buried two inches deep from the shower."

"Our trip back to New York brought us to many other islands far from St. Pierre, and everywhere we dropped anchor we heard more stories about the great eruption. Ships up to 400 miles away from the volcano reported ash falling on their decks. Two million tons of Pelee's dust fell on the island of Barbados 200 miles from St. Pierre. Everywhere the sea was dirty with floating ash and pumice. There were even earthquakes in Florida, but the most fantastic story of all was told to me by Captain Eric Lillienskjold of the Danish steamship Nordby, which had heard of no eruption and thought the world was coming to an end. Even more than the earthquakes in Florida and the ash on Barbados, the Nordby's experience showed me just how widespread was the volcanic disturbance that almost took my life."

Pelee erupted for 200 days. At the height of its power, the volcano was discharging 40 million cubic feet per minute, tossing a million feet of stone a minute for every life it took at St. Pierre. There has never been another eruption quite like it." But there have been others just as amazing as we will see, but first Mt. Pelee's mysterious neighbor, the Bermuda Triangle.

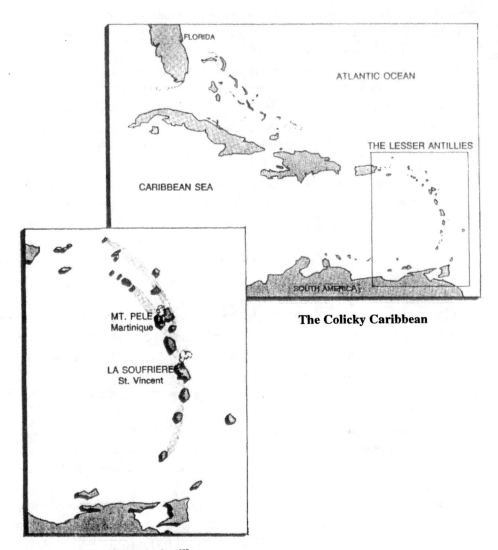

The Colicky Caribbean

The Volcanic Antilles

CHAPTER VIII

THE BERMUDA TRIANGLE

The Bermuda Triangle lies at the intersection of the two globe girdling volcano belts (the Alpine – Himilayan and the Circum – Pacific). Most of what has happened there can be explained through volcanic actions.

Eyewitness accounts of the Bermuda Triangle mysteries are legion. One that we can prove is related to volcanoes is the following. As in most of the experiences where someone lived to tell the tale, there was the spinning compass, triangular waves coming in all directions and the sudden dropping of the ship, peculiar features common only to volcano eruptions and the mysteries of the Triangle.

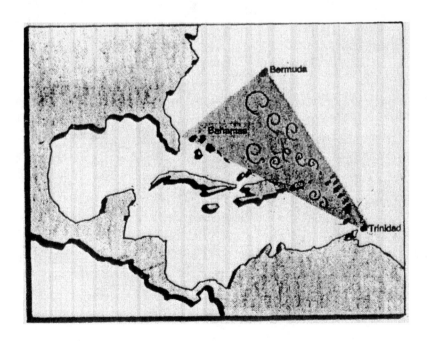

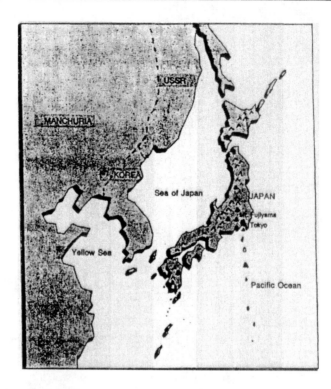

Japan is a string of 500 volcanoes worn like 'pearls on a smoking throat'

"Waves Without Wind and Lightning Without Thunder"
The Bermuda Triangle Strikes Again

One good example of a ship captain who thought the Triangle was haunted is the experience of Captain Eric Lillienskjold of the Danish ship Nordby. Lillienskjold knew nothing of the two great Caribbean volcanoes that erupted one day apart in 1902. He was many miles from either, but he was mighty relieved on landing in New York to find out there might be an explanation for what had happened to his haunted ship and his crew.

"On May 5th,' said Captain Lillienskjold, 'We touched at St. Michael's for water. We had had an easy voyage, sulfur-laden, from Girgenti, in Sicily, and we wanted to finish an easy run here (New York). We left St. Michael's on the same day. Nothing worth talking about occurred until two days afterward, Tuesday, May 7th."

"We were plodding along slowly that day. About noon I took the bridge to make an observation. It seemed to be hotter than ordinary. I shed my coat and vest and got into what little shade there was. As I worked, it grew hotter and hotter. I didn't know what to make of it."

"Along about two o'clock in the afternoon, it was so hot that all hands got to talking about it. All had heard of the Bermuda Triangle and knew we were within its boundaries.

We reckoned that something queer was happening to us, but none of us could explain what it was. You could almost see the pitch softening in the seams of the old ship."

"Then, as quick as you could toss a biscuit over its rail, the Nordby dropped – literally dropped – three or four feet down into the sea. No sooner had it done this then big triangular waves which looked as if they were coming from all directions at once, began to smash against our sides."

"This was queerer still, because the water a minute before had been as smooth as I had ever seen it, I had all hands piped on deck, and we battened down everything loose to make ready for a storm. And we got it all right – the strangest storm you ever heard of."

"There was something wrong with the sun that afternoon. It grew red and then dark red and then about a quarter after two, it went out of sight altogether. The day got so dark that you couldn't see half a ship's length ahead of you. We got our lamps going, and put on our oilskins, ready for a hurricane."

"All of a sudden there came a sheet of lightning that showed up the whole tumbling sea for miles and miles. We sort of ducked, expecting an awful crash of thunder, but it didn't come. There was no sound except the big waves pounding against our sides."

"There wasn't a breath of wind. Well, sir, at that minute there began the most exciting time I've ever been through, and I've been on every sea on the map in the past twenty-five years. Every second there would be waves fifteen or twenty feet high belting us head-on, stern-on and broadside, all at once. We could see them coming, for without any stop at all, flash after flash of lightning was blazing all about us."

"Something else we could see, too. Shark! There were hundreds of them on all sides, jumping up and down in the water. Some of them jumped clear out of it. And sea birds! A flock of them, squawking and crying made for our rigging and perched there. It seemed as if they were scared to death."

"But the queerest part of all was the water itself. It was hot – not so hot that our feet could not stand it when it washed over the deck – but hot enough to make us think that it had been heated by some kind of fire. Well, that sort of thing went on hour after hour. The waves, the lightning, the hot water and the sharks, and all the rest of the odd things happening, frightened the crew out of their wits."

"Some of them prayed out loud – I guess the first time they ever did in their lives. Some Frenchman aboard kept running around and yelling, 'C'est le denier jour!' (This is Judgment Day.) We were all worried. Even the officers began to think that the world was coming to an end. Mighty strange things happen on the sea, but this topped them all."

"I kept to the bridge all night. When the first hour of morning came, the storm was still gong on. We were all rather tired out by that time, but there was no such thing as trying to sleep. The waves were still batting us about, and we didn't know whether we were one mile or a thousand miles from shore. Our compass spun madly so it was impossible to get any reading."

"At two o'clock in the morning, all the queer goings-on stopped just the way they began – all of a sudden. We lay until daylight; then we took our reckonings and started off again. We were about 700 miles of Cape Henlopen. No, sir you couldn't get me through a thing like that again for $10,000. None of us was hurt, and the old Nordby herself pulled through all right; but I'd sooner stay ashore than see waves without wind, and lightning without thunder."

"On the 20th day of May, I landed once more in New York. I found it hard to believe the last twelve days had really happened on this earth. The horrors of my experience were beyond my comprehension, and I am afraid I have not told much of how it really was, as my mind will not let me remember it all."

Because of the dates, we know that the Nordby's near miss with the Bermuda Triangle was caused at least in part by the two great volcanic eruptions on Martinique and on St. Vincent. It raises the distinct possibility that all Triangle mysteries are caused by the effects from undersea submarine eruptions common in this area. The bottom of the Bermuda Triangle is covered with sea mounts which are either active or extinct volcano cones, according to Big John McLaughlin, the Navy hard hat diver and movie stunt man who held the sharks and doubled for Sean Connery and Lloyd Bridges on underwater shots in the James Bond movies and on the Sea Hunt television series. Big John, who lives in Fort Lauderdale, has his own Bermuda Triangle near miss experience.

"It was in 1959. We were sailing the Ft. George owned by the Hempstead's in Miami. We were bringing a 120 foot barge with bulldozers and front loaders from Jamaica to St. Thomas and were on our way back to Florida from the lower Bahamas. I had just finished my 12 to 6 am watch and lay down to sleep, with a gorgeous sun on its way up. I could tell it was going to be a super clear, flat summer day.

About two hours later, the other two crew members woke me and said something was wrong. I got up, and as we looked back behind the tug, a peculiar yellowish fog was there, and we couldn't see the barge. The fog was about 1000 feet back (we weren't in it, only the barge). Since we had no radio contact and only a compass, we checked the line which was pulling tight, but we still couldn't see the barge. According to our RDF (Radio direction finder), we weren't moving, so we pulled and pulled and increased power, but still the RDF said we weren't moving. The tug was going like crazy, the line was tight as a drum. We pulled for two to three hours like this, but still weren't going anywhere. Then, all of a sudden, the fog disappeared, and we started moving forward again."

There are certain common characteristics of volcano eruptions and incidents in the Bermuda Triangle to say nothing of the Dragon's Rectangle, which is exactly half way around the world from the Bermuda Triangle. In every big eruption, there are stories of spinning magnetic compasses gone wild just as this seems to occur on most of the ships and planes that survive or radio out pre-disappearance reports of odd things going on in the Triangle. The Bermuda Triangle is the second most explosive area in the world, and the Dragon's Rectangle, southwest from Japan, is the first. Both are close to great island based volcanoes such as Mt. Pelee on Martinique and Sulphatura on St. Vincent, the two most explosive Caribbean volcanoes, and the Central American land based eruption giants in Nicaragua, Costa Rica, Guatemala, Mexico and El Salvador. These Triangle bordering giants of destruction are seen, heard and felt in odd ways by the whole world, regionally they often completely change the configuration of the sea bottom many miles from their eruptions, changes that produce shoals that were never present on any charts. It is the extremely deep ocean trenches, however with their far more numerous submarine and sea mount volcanoes about which we know little except that they are perhaps the most influential factors in the peculiar events of the Bermuda Triangle.

For example, the reports of triangular waves coming every which way all at once, the boiling seas, spinning compasses and the peculiar dry yellow fog are all volcanic characteristics of underwater as well as above water eruptions. Almost all reports from ships and planes escaping the Triangle have confirmed these terrifying situations.

A simple experiment will show how a cork or model ship will sink "a few feet" deeper in "carbonated water" or any kind of water with air in it from turbulence so why wouldn't a heavily loaded ship coming on one of these dry fog eruptive spots have more trouble with flotation? The water is less dense and already heavily laden coal and ore shiploads become proportionately more dense than usual.

The yellowish dry fog that hides everything that penetrates into it is another common characteristic of volcanic eruption and the mysterious dry fogs that envelope ships and planes in the Triangle. Of course these incidents are rare, compared with all the vessels and planes which fly the area, but they are not all that uncommon in the Bermuda Triangle, butting on heavily populated Miami-Fort Lauderdale and the Dragon's Rectangle, siding on to Japan. Both areas, Florida in particular, have dense populations of pleasure boats and planes with amateur pilots and often questionable navigators.

Nevertheless, the statistics of boats and planes which have disappeared without a trace are mind boggling. So much for survivor stories...

In the 30 years between 1945 and 1975, there have been 67 ships and 192 aircraft of all sizes disappear in the Triangle with no explanation, plus many times that many ships sunk or nearly sank but where the disaster reason has been at least partially identified as poor navigation, bad luck, engine trouble or human error. The point is we are only concerned here with statistics of boats and planes where we cannot find an explanation or even a clue.

In the Dragon's Rectangle off Japan, evidence is even more dramatic. In one year (1968) 521 boats were missing from unknown causes (435 in 1970 and 471 in 1972). Charles Berlitz, questioning these figures from the Japanese Maritime Safety Agency, also notes a ship five times larger than the Titanic, The Berge Istra, 227,912 dead weight tons, disappeared in December, 1975, with two other huge ships, the English ship Darbyshire 169,044 DWT and South Korea's Hae Dang, 102,805 DWT, disappearing less than two months apart in 1980. The remains, if any, of these ships are gone without a trace. If they exist they must lie in very deep ocean trenches, much deeper than Everest is high.

At least two sizable Japanese scientific research vessels sent to investigate the large number of mysterious sinkings in the Dragon's Rectangle were also lost without a trace. The Kaio Muru #5, a 500 ton scientific vessel loaded with safety and rescue equipment, not to mention oceanographers and geologists in its crew of 30, also went down without a warning signal on September 24, 1952. Many surface war ships and dozens of submarines were lost in this Rectangle in WWII, but it is the smaller fishing ships that have been disappearing for centuries (when no war was involved) that add to the mystery.

The aforementioned Japanese Maritime Safety Agency ship Kaio Muru #5 is the only ship that left any real clues in a search of the entire area of thousands of miles. A few pieces of debris were found with pumice flakes clinging to them, which led the Marine science agency to speculate that the ship had overturned and sunk during submarine volcano eruption, logical but far from conclusive evidence of why this ship disappeared without an SOS.

As mysterious as the eerie disappearance of sea vessels in the Triangle, there seems to be a more plausible explanation of how the ships sank than the hundreds of air craft which were also victims of the Bermuda Triangle. Here are three examples, the first is by the world's most famous pilot and his plane which luckily hangs in the Smithsonian instead of having disappeared somewhere in the Bermuda Triangle.

The story is quoted from the famous pilot's last book *Autobiography of Values*, as passed on in the third person by Martin Caidin in *Ghosts of the Air*.

"The pilot departed Havana, Cuba at 1:35 A.M. on a long planned flight direct to Saint Louis, Missouri. He planned to cross the Straits of Florida and then continue on to his destination. Most of his flying would be dead reckoning. This was 1928, and the navigation aids we take for granted today weren't even wishful thinking in those times. But the pilot was as resourceful as he was well experienced.

As he left Cuba behind and flew over open water, "strange things" began to happen inside and to his plane. They made no sense, and they baffled him. First, his magnetic compass began to turn to the right, then to the left, right again, left again, and suddenly it began to rotate around and around. It was spinning uselessly. It wasn't supposed to do that. A magnetic compass can be affected to give an "off" reading, but they don't spin madly so that they're completely useless. Every now and then a pilot would talk about his mag compass "going wild" or "berserk" and spinning so fast it would even break its container bowl and splash alcohol over the instrument panel. That was almost the situation now.

But not to worry. This aircraft also had an earth induction indicator, about as solid a piece of navigation equipment for its time as one could obtain. You could use the EII for crossing oceans, and many pilots used them for more reliable long-range navigation. But now the EII in this plane went bananas; it began to wander erratically, pointing first one way, and then indicating a course to follow that made absolutely no sense.

In short, both compasses were now useless. The pilot had no way to use those instruments to check his heading, or to use timing and dead reckoning to figure his position.

But he was good. He kept flying as steadily as he could, using star references to hold course. Soon that also went to hell in a hand basket. Haze settled like an instant mist through the entire area. Fog formed to blind the pilot. Above him the stars were now barely visible, and beyond use as navigational reference.

So the pilot went down low, as low as he dared in the dark. He figured that by judging the whitecaps of waves, their size and movement and direction, he would have at least a rough idea of the wind direction, its force, and if it had changed from the forecasts. That didn't work; the air became turbulent, it was difficult to see out of the plane.

Dawn finally began to streak the eastern horizon. The pilot couldn't believe the sky. He later described it as looking like 'dark milk.'

The sun kept pushing up and the sky brightened so that now he could see the surface below. He was over land! And his compass was starting, just as crazily as it had gone bad before, to reverse its wild behavior. It settled down and now worked perfectly. So did the earth induction indicator.

It took a while for the pilot to locate his position. For several minutes he scanned the shoreline features, and then his charts. If they matched, as they seemed to do, then he was far off course. So far that it exceeded any distance he could possibly have reached with the fuel on board. The rest of his trip back to St. Louis was uneventful.

THE LOST PILOT? CHARLES A. LINDBERGH, "LUCKY LINDY," FLYING HIS FAMOUS SINGLE ENGINE MONOPLANE THE SPIRIT OF SAINT LOUIS IN 1928.

Our second flying experience has a happy ending. It also comes courtesy of Caidin and his *Ghosts of the Air*. It is quoted from Royal Air Force pilot John Hawks who probably clocked even more miles in his career then Lucky Lindy. John Hawks was flying an Aztec, equipped with long range gas tanks from Fort Lauderdale Executive Airport to Bermuda.

"I was on autopilot, everything as neat as a pin, and I'd crossed the drink a few hundred times already. It was like being at home. Everything was perfect until I found myself staring at the mag compass. I was staring at it, all right, but I couldn't see the stupid thing.

Oh, the compass was still there. But that compass card, that idiot thing, was spinning so fast, it was a blur. And I began feeling as if I were passing out. Like slipping under an anesthetic.

That's not the time to contemplate; it's the time to do. First thing I did was push my seat way back. If I was going to slop around that cabin like a sack of grain, I didn't want to fall on the yoke. Puts you right in the water, raises your insurance premiums, and ruins the flight, right?

So back I go with the seat and think I really ought to up the trim a bit to compensate. Change of CG and all that. But I couldn't do it. Weak as a kitten.

I put my head back on the rest and had a good look at the sky. It wasn't there. Just creamy yellow everywhere. No clouds, no water, no horizon, no blue. Just yellow. And I'm passing out. Last thing I did before I went down the tube was look at my watch. My arm felt like lead, but I fixed the numbers in my head, and the lights went out. I came back to things just one hour later." Obviously John Hawks made it back, but not so the six pilots and crews in the next Bermuda horror.

It is perhaps the most famous, the most searched for and the most investigated case of planes disappearing in the Triangle without a trace. Let us see if we can match it up with some volcanic happenings we know occurred with eruptions both above and below the sea. In this case, not one but six planes in two flights disappeared without a trace at the tail end of WWII.

The date was December 5, 1945. Flight 19, five TBM Navy Avenger Fighter Bombers with three men crews and with the latest radio communication and navigation equipment. The planes took off on a routine mid afternoon training exercise with good visibility from their Fort Lauderdale Naval Training Base. Each plane had an experienced pilot in charge. The flight plan called for a triangular course 160 miles east, then 40 miles north over Grand Bahama Island then southwest right back to their Fort Lauderdale base. They took off at 2:02 p.m. and were flying in formation at a speed of 200 miles per hour. The planes appeared to be in perfect order mechanically.

Lt. Charles C. Taylor piloted the lead plane on what appeared was going to be a milk run. One and a half hours into the flight when they should have been almost home, Lt. Taylor radioed in that both his compasses were malfunctioning. We must assume the other planes were having a similar problem getting an accurate compass reading. The control tower in Fort Lauderdale could hear the planes talking to each other. The radio conversation with the flight was weird calling the tower. "This is an emergency. We seem to be off course... We cannot see land... (repeat) We cannot see land..." The tower asked the commander for his position. He replied, "We are not sure of our position. We can't be sure. We seem to be lost." The tower told the flight to head due west. The flight commander replied, "We don't know which way is west. Everything is wrong... strange. We can't be sure of any direction. Even the ocean doesn't look as it should." Then for some unknown reason, 15 minutes later, the tower heard the men talking among themselves.

Confusing messages continued to come in and four hours into the flight and two hours over due, Taylor announced they would try to land their planes on the water together as they were almost out of gas. "Looks like we are–" and no further sound was ever heard again from Flight 19. A Martin flying boat with a crew of 13 men took off on a rescue mission to try and find Flight 19. Five minutes later it, too, vanished.

The Coast Guard searched for the six missing planes all night long, joined in the morning by more planes from an aircraft carrier. The search party swelled to 21 ships, 300 planes and 12 land based parties combing the Everglades. The five day search covered a 250,000 mile area. Not even the 400 page report of a Naval Inquiry Board could answer questions such as "Why was there no SOS and no debris? Why didn't the Martin Flying Boat land on the water and what happened to its emergency radio equipment?" The report concluded with complete frustration "We are not able to make even a good guess as to what happened."

The scientific world continues to speculate as do my many friends who live on the Florida side of the Triangle so I add my guesses here. First, we must look to volcanoes (and to my knowledge nobody has ever done that). Several of the mysterious reports on Flight 19 and certainly other Triangle mystery cases have had all or several of the following volcanic conditions in common. (1) Magnetic compasses spinning out of control. (2) The area covered by a dense yellow fog which we must assume comes from submarine volcanoes. The fog was giving off eye burning sulfuric acid and various other poison gases such as nitrous oxide, the laughing gas my old "painless dentist" used to give me when he went after a bad tooth. (It was nitrous oxide that affected John Hawk in our previous mystery case.) Another common volcanic gas is the highly inflammable methane (the flame you see coming from the side of your sewer plant.)

Since military pilots are generally quite curious and daring, we can assume that seeing a local patch of low hanging (volcanic gases are heavy) yellow clouds drifting in an otherwise cloudless sky, the lead pilot might have flown in to investigate.

Once into the cloud, and these five planes were flying in formation, the sparks from the piston engine instantly exploded the methane gas and all the planes went up at once. A methane explosion can be so great that nothing larger than tiny coin sized chips would be left of the air craft and these would quickly sink and be swallowed by sea bottom muck and sand.

So, believe it or not, the methane theory is logical and has yet to be disproven as most of the earlier Bermuda Triangle evidence has been tested and abandoned.

The important point here, regardless of whether we have a solution to the mystery of the Triangle, is that volcanoes (rather than fossil fuels or man made CFC's) have had the major hand in the mysterious disappearances of the Bermuda Triangle.

Enough of this speculation. I promised a book explaining with volcano facts about our global climate so back to reality and the world's deepest active volcano crater and the largest eruption of the 20th Century right here in North America.

Looking down into Katmai, the largest active crater in the world.

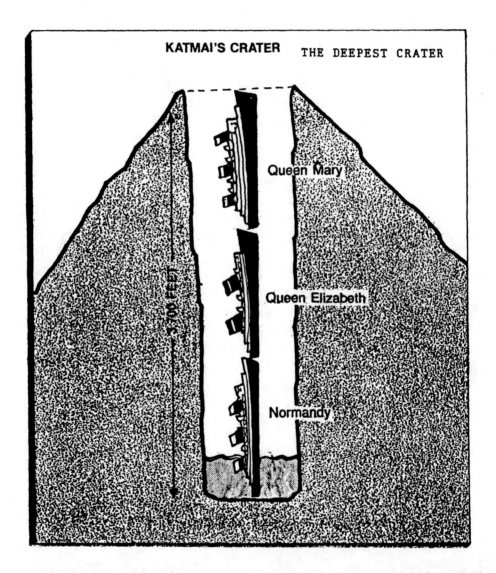

KATMAI'S CRATER THE DEEPEST CRATER

Queen Mary

Queen Elizabeth

Normandy

Katmai has the world's deepest crater so deep that the three ocean liners, Queen Mary, Queen Elizabeth I and the Normandy could stand end to end and not reach the 3,700 foot bottom (nearly 3/4 mile straight down). The crater is also three miles across the top. If Mark Twain found Vesuvius a mere toy beside Kilauea, he would have found Katmai far wider and many times as deep.

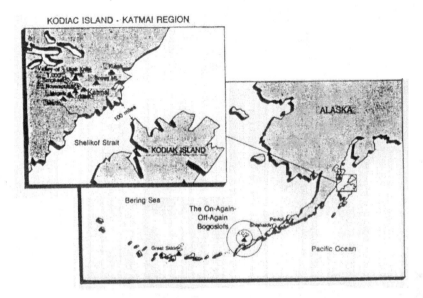

Alaska and Aleutian archipelago volcano chain
(Part of the Circum-Pacific Ring of Fire)

Acid rain is real, but it doesn't come out of industry's smokestacks in any great quantity...
In Seattle, 1600 miles from Katmai on June 6 (D-Day) 1912, the acid rain attacked wash
lines, causing clothes to fall apart on the ironing board. One irate housewife demanded that
her grocer write the soap company for an explanation.

CHAPTER IX

KATMAI (1912)
NORTH AMERICA'S BIGGEST ERUPTION

The remains of Katmai.

North America's greatest historic eruption (at least 12 times as powerful as St. Helens) was thoroughly documented as to its peculiar individuality, during and after the eruption in 1912 by Robert Griggs and his team from the National Geographical Society. The volcano was in such a remote area of Alaska that it took three years to reach the crater.

Katmai's eruption on June 6, 1912 was a D-day many times as explosive as Normandy, although it was so far from civilization no one was killed and very few even heard the blast. It was one of the dozen greatest explosions on record, the greatest of the twentieth century, and by far the most powerful since records have been kept in North

American history. The crater it left in the jagged remnants of a once-beautiful snow-capped cone is deeper than any other in the world.

The difference between Katmai mountain as it now stands, and as it was before the top disappeared, is over two cubic miles, more than 40 times the excavations of the Panama Canal. The total ejecta from the eruption was nearly seven cubic miles of sand, ash and lava. It would take all the stone crushers in the United States 500 years to match the brief production of Katmai's one eruption. The vast quantities of dust it threw into the air obscured so much of the sunlight usually thawing out the sub-polar lands and oceans that 1912 was the coldest summer in North American history. Yet the volcano stayed hot for so long and was so far off any beaten path that it was more than three years before anyone reached the crater rim to establish it as the definite source of the explosion. (The 1915 National Geographic Society Expedition led by Robert F. Griggs.)

Scenes at Kodiak, an island 100 miles from Katmai

Photograph by W. J. Erskine

The end of the ash fall at Kodiak

At first the ash was comparatively soft and fluffy. Later it settled down into a hard compact layer ten inches thick.

Photograph by W. J. Erskine

Ash pile from a roof, Kodiak
It looks very much like snow as it lies on the ground but, being in reality pulverized rock of great weight, it did much damage.

This eruption was so powerful that its dust clouded the sun over Algeria, retarded the growth of corn in Wisconsin and cost Seattle housewives money as it ruined their clothes 1600 miles from the volcano.

Katmai was just a name on the sea charts along treacherous, seldom-traveled Shilikof Strait in the Alaskan peninsula, until it buried Kodiak, 100 miles away, in a foot of rock dust and inflicted a total blackout on the island for 60 hours at a season when Kodiak is supposed to have daylight 21 hours a day. Ironically if it happened today, it would be used as an excuse to ban all air conditioners, fire places and wood burning stoves and barbecues, yet all the cars in the land burning fossil fuels are an insignificant 3% of the output of one volcano, less than one-quarter the size of Katmai.

Inhabitants of Kodiak, a non-volcanic island in a non-volcanic region of Alaska, could not have been more surprised by their fate if they had been New Yorkers suddenly cast into darkness and buried in pulverized stone thrown from one of the extinct volcanoes in Connecticut.

The natives of Kodiak had never before heard thunder, and they were not used to the clinkers and dirt that every New Yorker must scrape out of his eyes at one time or another. The eruption brought both these phenomena in quantity as well as many more. As Katmai's heavy black cloud smothered Kodiak like a short-circuited electric blanket, there was nothing visible in the heavy blackness except thousands of tiny lightning flashes in a hopeless tangle of fuzzy, golden threads, like lint under a microscope. Rooftops were caved under a foot of rock snow and darkness was so impenetrable into the third day that a lighted lantern could not be seen at arm's length. There was panic in the streets as dust-choked men knocked heads on their way to fortify themselves with whiskey in the dusty, flour-white saloons.

Kodiak is an outstanding example of human terror when the minds of men do not understand the source of discomfort. Whereas most volcanic eruptions begin with weeks of minor outbursts and lull their victims into careless confidence until it is too late, Kodiak was in a constant state of hysteria from no danger at all. People who could have stayed in their homes with only minor discomforts, fled instead to the sea, sure that doom would strike them down at any moment. Grizzled prospectors, Eskimo trappers, Indian squaws with their papooses; a polyglot mixture of every race, color and as many smells, crowded 500 strong onto a ship (the revenue cutter "Manning"), capable of accommodating only 100 people. It was a floating "black hole" of whiskey breath, tobacco juice and perspiration inspired by hazy recollections of the vivid horrors of St. Pierre and Pompeii.

Although a few anxious citizens were bruised and stepped on in the swirling eddies of volcanic dust and heavy darkness, the only real damage in Kodiak was to property. An avalanche of talc-like stone slid down the mountainside behind Kodiak, picking up weight and speed as it fell. It choked and buried homes already top-heavy with ash that had snowed down from the ebony, lightning-cracked sky.

Kodiak was but one sufferer in a wide arc of cities, towns and ships which noted the spreading phenomena of Katmai's eruption.

While the explosions were not heard at Kodiak, they were well within earshot of Iliamna Bay, 115 miles northeast of the volcano. Eskimos there reported hearing distant booming after which there was a sudden shift of clouds in the sky. A fisherman said the clouds above his trawler quivered like the mirror in his mine shack during a dynamite blast. The eruption was also heard at Juneau, 750 miles away from the crater.

The Associated Press at Seward, 250 miles from the volcano, reported a slight rain on June 11, "which is killing all vegetation and eating into the metal work of buildings."

Photograph by George C. Martin

A field of floating pumice from Katmai in Amalik Bay
The boat could not be rowed farther into it. Fishermen reported a similar field in Shilikof Strait dense enough to support a man. It floated indefinitely. Considerable quantities were still encountered a year after the eruption.

In Cape Spencer, 700 miles east of the blast, this same sulphuric acid rain tarnished brass on the deck of a steamship every fifteen minutes – completely frustrating the bewildered sailor ordered to keep it polished.

Acid rain reached the Puget Sound area 1500 miles away from the crater, and attacked clothes hanging on a Seattle wash-line. They later fell apart on the ironing board before the disbelieving eyes of a housewife who demanded that her grocer write the soap company for an explanation.

At Kaflia Bay, only thirty miles from Katmai but protected by mountains, Ivan Orloff wrote his wife describing "ashes six to ten feet deep", and told her he was "awaiting death any moment". He lived and was unharmed although half buried in ash.

Katmai's ash fell at least a foot thick over an area one and one-half times the size of Delaware, and dust, 1600 miles from its source, sprinkled Seattle, Washington. In Victoria, British Columbia, sulphuric acid ash strong enough to sting the eyes and skin fell for thirty hours.

Before it settled down, the volcano had cast out 28,000,700 tons of pulverized rock, part of which floated for years on nearby lakes and bays as porous ash paste strong and rubbery enough to support a man.

This bombardment of Nature upon nature, which man witnessed only indirectly, went on for weeks before and after June 6, but the three most violent explosions, corresponding to the three different layers of ashfall on Kodiak, came at 3:00 p.m. and 11:00 p.m., June 6, and 10:40 p.m. on June 7. The eruption continued in a milder state all summer, its fiery crater reflecting red on the black clouds of smoke and obscuring the top of the mountain which no one was around to see.

On July 19, 1916 Professor Robert F. Griggs and his National Geographic Society associates first reached the crater of Katmai after an arduous climb over slippery mud flows and treacherous ash-covered glaciers. They found the rim of the crater still as "sharp as a gabled roof". They came on it so suddenly that the lead man almost walked into the abyss.

Only by lying on their stomachs and edging up to the knife-sharp rim could the explorer-scientists look over the edge with semi-safety. They saw sheer, multi-colored cliffs rimmed on top by blue-ice glaciers and descending an unfathomable 3,700 feet. At the bottom was a beautiful Alpine lake of milky blue with a crescent island in its middle. Columns of steam hissed around the island as if it was a hot horseshoe dipped in a smithy's water bucket. There were yellow sulphur deposits, black, brown, red and grey rock and white snow fields at the bottom of the crater opposite the lake. The explorers found it impossible to describe the effect or measure the mammoth size of the crater, especially when trying to project their thinking to the original 4,200-foot height of Katmai Mountain. Even the cut down version was and is the deepest crater and perhaps the deepest hole in the world. It defies size estimates because of perfect proportions. The crater finally surveyed was eight and one-half miles around the rim and three-quarters of a mile almost straight down. This depth is equivalent to the world's three longest ocean liners (the Queen Elizabeth, the Queen Mary, and the Normandy), if stood end-to-end atop each other. The crater from its rim to the bottom of the lake would hold 900,000 million gallons of water – enough to supply thirsty New York City for four years.

THE DEEPEST CRATER
A Flood of Hot Sand

The results of Katmai's great eruption are spelled out here as examples of what volcanoes and only volcanoes can do to affect the environment. They are NOT listed to show what man will do if he doesn't stop polluting the environment but rather to show how enormous nature's effects can be compared with the completely insignificant impact of man's indulgences. The reader may disagree, but surely this disagreement will not make the reading any less amazing and interesting. Once again, we go to the National Geographic Expedition nearly four years after the eruption for our factual narrative.

One aspect of the Katmai upheaval is different from all other known eruptions. Almost two cubic miles of hot sand poured out of the ground in a relentless wave, like slow-moving molasses. It filled the mouth of a valley like a thick, searing tongue nine miles wide and 15 miles long. 137 square miles were covered 500 feet deep in burning quick sand which, like the hottest lava flows, turned everything it touched to charcoal.

Oddly enough, this sand did not come from Katmai Crater, but flowed out of the valley bottom filling it like a spring-fed lake.

If all these burning sands were poured into a barrel around New York, every lobby and elevator shaft in the city would be stuffed solid with it. Only the tips of the Empire State, Chrysler and Trade Center buildings would protrude, providing these buildings were wrapped in thick layers of asbestos.

The heat would be so intense in sand-drowned Manhattan that it would be several months before anyone could come closer than Patterson, New Jersey; and in Patterson, bakers might turn out their daily supply of fresh bread by putting the raw loaves into an outside fumarole, one of ten thousand smokes in Jersey meadows.

ALL NEW WATER COMES FROM VOLCANOES
The Katmai Flood

In 1912 Alaska had a flood 35 times more destructive than Johnstown, PA. and a million times the force of the Mississippi's most devastating flood. Katmai, North America's most explosive volcano mountain is not an ash cone as are most volcanoes, but a series of layers of old lava humped up on top of each other like felt hats over a blocking dummy. Some time during Katmai's 1912 eruption earthshaking vibrations caused an enormous sheet of this prehistoric lava to break loose from the side of the mountain and flake off in a thundering landslide. The lava crashed into a narrow canyon of the Katmai River at the exact spot an engineer would have selected as the most effective dam site. This volcano-built dam backed up 8,000 million cubic feet of water, 400 feet deep and covering 950 acres.

Filling the lake behind this huge reservoir took three years, but the job was not quite perfect, and as pressure built up behind the dam, seepage worked its way through the loose gravel under the head-wall and eroded its foundation. When this amazing volcano-dam could no longer hold back the ever-increasing weight of the water, it did not spring a leak as most dams would, but slid off its mountings as a solid wall, and raced down Katmai Canyon (4,000 feet deep) and out into the lower valley. There were 60 billion gallons of solid water pushing it relentlessly from the rear.

This irrepressible mountain of water was released with such sudden fury that it did not even have time to seek its own level. At one point where the furious water was supposed to go around a ridge, it couldn't make the turn and went over the top in a waterfall as great as Niagara. At the ridge, the bottom of the onrushing stream was 40 feet higher than its bank which was still dry. Like the swirling drainage when the plug in a bathtub is pulled, the centrifugal force of the racing torrents became greater than the local weight of the water. Unable to make the wide-angle turn, it swelled up and over the ridge like an enormous lopsided whirlpool.

When it came out onto the flat valley floor, the raging flood was moving so fast that it deposited huge cobblestones on top of light ash it did not take time to disturb.

The violence of the deluge was so great that trees were not uprooted but sheared off at their base. A hundred-ton lava boulder was carried a mile and one-half. There were hundreds of rocks at least ten feet in diameter moved along in front of the flood with such velocity that they knocked down everything in their path.

The flood was still moving fast enough when it passed over Katmai Village, evacuated by necessity and law since the eruption, to move the half-buried houses and stuff the church to its steeple-top with mud. The heavy-laden waters filled Katmai Bay with silt and left it strewn with treacherous tree stumps.

The Great Hot Sandflow of the Valley

Photograph by P. R. Hagelbarger

The Deepest Crater
A flood of hot sand. Looking across the sandflow near its terminus.

By comparison with the USA's better-known floods closer to home, the Katmai torrents were 35 times as destructive as those which drowned 10,000 people at Johnstown, Pennsylvania, on May 31, 1889. Both floods were caused by the bursting of a dam. The force behind the Johnstown disaster was so great that a man standing in a third-story window saw a locomotive "come dancing along the top of the flood thirty feet off the ground," yet the Katmai flood had 12 and one-half times as much water with three times the fall giving it a total energy 35 times as great as Johnstown.

The Katmai deluge also had one million times the force of the most destructive flood in the Mississippi River's history. Contrary to popular opinion about Mississippi floods moving at jet-propelled speed, the top flood current velocity of the river is only about ten feet per second. Katmai's was ten times this speed! Since water's destructive capacity is increased as the sixth power of its velocity, Katmai's force was a million times greater than the Mississippi's flood power at any given moment.

Ghost Forests and Talking Mountains

Ash from Alaska's Katmai was thrown so high that it cooled before it came to earth, even within sight of the cone. As a result, one of the most grotesque experiences in the volcano area is a ghost forest of spooky white cottonwood trees. The trees were choked to death with ash, but they never burned as did everything the sand flow touched in the nearby valley of "Ten Thousand Smokes."

Dust storms in the forest whipped the National Geographic Expedition men with stinging sand, and in one spot the wind rolled gravel at them like fast-moving marbles, sometimes raising the stones off the ground to pelt victims as if they were being assaulted by half-spent minie balls fired from a cannon. On several occasions the terrible wind blew down the expedition's "windproof" camp, and one night picked Professor Griggs (head man of the expedition) up off the ground, throwing him 40 feet into a warm volcanic mud bank which he clutched for dear life.

Snowdrifts buried by ash in the ghost forest remained frozen for years like white pieces of marshmallow baked in a chocolate cake. In other spots warmed by hot volcanic soil, there were caverns left by snows melting under the thick pumice covering. The danger of cave-ins from these dripping underground tombs left little peace of mind for the explorers traversing the cavern roof tops, especially with the eerie, dead trees standing guard in a silent, grey world where nothing lives or moves.

Griggs also reported a moving mountain in the upper Katmai Valley which never stops its wanderings; called "Noisy Mountain," it livened up the night for the men camped near its base with angry rock falls every five minutes. In its greatest slide the whole side of Noisy Mountain flaked off and slid into the upper Katmai Valley, burying several miles in debris and leaving a raw, jagged escarpment 150 feet high, as a sliding board for future deluges. On top of the initial load smaller slides still build their burial mounds ranging from a single boulder to piles 300 ft. high.

There are two kinds of noises which give "Noisy Mountain" its name. One is the low, terrifying rumble that precedes an earthquake, and the second is the "boom, rattle, bang" of rolling rocks bouncing down a cliff.

In the bigger slides, those causing the earthquake-type rumble, over 100 cubic yards of rubble crashes 1500 feet into the valley floor. These rockslides are caused by a periodic flushing of sun-melted snows piling up behind the gravel, dirt and ash choking their run-off paths. The falling mixture of these water slides is a poor grade concrete containing everything from pumice, water, mud and sand to three-foot boulders.

Aleuts, Bears and Salmon

No discussion of Katmai would be complete without a description of the people who once lived in the forests of this now desolate area. They are descendants of the fierce

Aleut Indians who gave the Russians so much trouble after Vitus Bering opened "Russian America" for fur trade in 1741. The name "A-la-as-ka" means "the great country" in Aleut. The "great" people found there when the Russians arrived had little or no beard, black eyes, short neck and stocky body.

They were fierce defenders of their homes and customs. They believed in mummifying their dead, which they did by removing the intestines and stuffing the body with dry, scented grass. The bodies were then suspended by their long, black hair from the roof of a moss burial cave so that they could swing easily in the wind and join each other in some spiritual communion.

The Aleuts also believed in communal cave dwelling while still alive. Their homes were large, half-buried sod houses called barabaras. Some of these accommodated ten to 40 families and were up to 240 feet long and 40 feet wide. Heat and light were provided by stone lamps burning oil from whales killed with spears. The stone spear heads, each different so as to identify the owner, were dipped in poison and thrust into the whale, which died in two or three days and floated ashore.

Aleut men wore long skirts of feathered birdskins, and fur stockings. Their hooded raincoats were made of seal intestines, tied at the face and wrists with sinew drawstring. Women were tattooed on the face and wore ornaments piercing their ears, lips and nose. These Indians dieted almost entirely on raw food; meat, whale and seal blubber with raw eggs and green stuff added in the short summer season.

There are many stories of "savage" raids by the Aleuts, but population figures would indicate that the early white adventurers had all the better of these fights for survival. When the Russians first began exploiting the Aleutian archipelago for furs, there were 25,000 Aleuts, but by 1890 their census numbered less than a thousand.

The inhabitants of the Katmai area are descendants of the Aleuts. They once made "blood-thirsty" attacks on the white settlement near Naknek Lake, killing all but one man who escaped by hiding under a waterfall.

The Aleuts still do not think much of the settlement at Naknek, judging from the opinion of "American Pete", Chief of the Savonoski village, whose prelude report on the Katmai eruption is the nearest thing to an eye-witness account.

"The Katmai Mountain she blew up. Lots of fire. Fire come down trail... lots of smoke. We go fast Savonski. Everybody get in bidarka (skin boat). Work like hell. Helluva job. We come Naknek one day. Dark – no could see. Hot ash fall down. Work like hell.

"Now go back every year, one month maybe, after fish, all dry and kill bear. Too bad. Never can go back Savonoski live again. Everything ash. Good place, too, you bet once. Fine trees, lots moose, mar, deer. Lots fish front of barabara (dugout sod house). No many mosquitos. Fine church. Fine house. Naknek no good."

If the Aleuts do not like Naknek, and gave up on Katmai as a home, the sockeye salmon are more persistent. Even an alive volcano choking their streams with ash cannot seem to stop them from getting there. The wonder of the salmon with their ability to leave a fresh water spawning area as young fish, swim out to the ocean and return to the exact spot of their birth in old age to breed and die is dramatically illustrated by those born the year of the eruption who returned years later through muddy, ash-filled streams only inches deep to jump waterfalls within sight of Katmai and get back to Naknek Lake.

There were monstrous problems for the four-legged animals around Katmai, too, although the eruption did not seem to scare the Alaska bear as much as it did other wildlife. Far from frightened by volcanic wonders, the 1500-pound bears, larger and more ferocious than lions and tigers, stopped regularly to warm themselves on the warm ground beside the steam geysers in crossing "The Valley of Ten Thousand Smokes," and left tracks and hair in the mud to prove it. The "Kodiak" bear around Katmai is the largest carnivorous animal in the world and has a reputation to uphold.

Not so lucky, nor so comfortable, were the large herds of reindeer roaming slopes above Katmai Pass. Everything green was covered by a layer of ash. When the reindeer grazed, their teeth were ground down by an abrasive pumice until they could no longer chew properly. They died by the hundreds, and what remained of the herds left the Katmai valleys to return five years later after the dust settled.

Photograph by R. F. Griggs

The main arm of the Valley of Ten Thousand Smokes
"No photograph can convey more than a slight conception of the wonder and majesty of
this sight as it first burst on our vision on crossing the pass." Robert F. Griggs, leader of the
National Geographic expedition which got to the Katmai pass in 1916.

The Valley of Ten Thousand Smokes

At the head of the second Katmai Valley, beyond the quicksand, the ghost forest and
the landslides, lies lofty Katmai pass perched between two active volcanoes – Trident
and Mageik, and close to the half-destroyed Katmai Mountain that once dominated the
skyline.

Even before volcanic disturbances added to the atmospheric confusion, this Pass had
a reputation for foul and dangerous weather unmatched in North America. Father
Hubbard, best known of the recent Alaskan explorers and volcano climbers, called this
area the most treacherous place in Alaska, if not the whole world.

The Indians had an inter-tribal trail over Katmai Pass for centuries. It cut off 300
miles going around the Alaskan peninsula. After sleeping overnight in Katmai Village,
prospectors left via the Pass on the shortest route to Nome in the gold stampede of 1898.

Sourdough Charlie Carter, who carried the mail from Nome to Katmai by dogsled,
noticed the ice on Naknek Lake (west of the Pass) sometimes thawed out when the air
was no more than fifteen degrees fahrenheit. He assumed there were hot springs. Carter
could not have imagined the volcanic activity, however, that American scientists Robert
F. Griggs and L.G. Folsom beheld when they first crossed the Katmai Pass in 1916.

Their unprecedented discovery was the strangest and newest of volcanic phenomena which they called, after their first impression, "The Valley of Ten Thousand Smokes" – an estimate they later revised to millions.

The panorama as far as their eyes could reach was full of curling smokes from tiny fumaroles to steam geysers a thousand feet high. Steam came out of a million vents, from tiny cracks to pits and craters 150 feet in diameter. Anywhere they punched a hole in the hot ground steam burst forth in a new "smoke". It was as though all the steam engines in the world, assembled together, had popped their safety valves at once and were letting off surplus steam in concert." The largest fumarole shot its cloud of white vapor 2000 feet into the air, higher than the mountains around it and plainly visible three miles away. There were thousands of other fumaroles no longer active that left brightly-colored minerals on the ground to add beauty to the valley's steaming fountain.

It was 10,000 small volcanoes coming up through a wall of flat sand in 50 square miles of continuous effusion. For ten years (1912-1922) there was more energy given off in this valley than by the sum total of all the other volcanoes in the Western Hemisphere, and certainly many times the total output by man.

In five years of exploration the National Geographic Society expedition members never got used to the place. It was like living on top a massive old boiler full of leaks, but still churning a record head of steam. They could not decide if it was "an Elysium or a Tartaras".

Everywhere in the enormous Y-shaped valley bounded by monster live volcanoes (Katmai, Trident, Martin, Mageik) 15 miles away, the explorers found hot ground which burned right through the thick soles of their workshoes if they did not keep moving, yet the ash floor over the hot, steaming sand was such a poor conductor that a spot which melted zinc a few inches below the ground at 1200 degrees was little more than air temperature at the surface.

Occasionally, a breath of steam blown over the group by an unpredictable wind, would give its victims an uncomfortable burn. A bit of sleepwalking or dreaming in this hypnotic land of fantasy, and a person could easily wander into a scalding funeral and never return. Even when wide awake, there was danger of breaking through the hollow crust and boiling to death. Imagination and fear work overtime in such surroundings, and it was several days before members of the expedition could lie down without fear of poison gas, cave-ins or some other strange death.

Yet the scientific wonders of the valley were not all uncomfortable. The expedition chose a campsite 250 feet above the valley floor that would have been a housewife's dream if she did not first die of fright from the mysterious appliances that were hers to use.

Just beyond the back door was a rent-free refrigerator and deep freeze; a glacier cave big enough and cold enough to satisfy any want and never in need of defrosting or repair.

A few yards in front of the house was a cookstove that had everything you could find in a modern hotel range from steam trays to gas jets, ovens and temperature control. Since the pots are surrounded by an atmosphere of live steam just at the point of condensing, nothing ever boils away, cooks to pieces, or burns no matter how long neglected or forgotten. Griggs tells of one case where they left oatmeal to cook two days and returned to find it as fresh, moist and palatable as an hour after they put it in the stove hole. Natural temperature control held the cereal exactly at the boiling point but never higher so that it might boil away. Beans dropped on the kitchen floor sprouted rapidly for those who like a Chinese menu replete with fresh bean sprouts. This was one steam hole, yet other "smokes" further away were hot enough to melt lead or zinc, and even turn aluminum soft enough to be cut with a knife. At the hottest hole, the scientists held a walking stick in the steam. It smoked violently and when drawn out became a glowing coal. Then they notched the end of the cane to make a fuzz stick and thrust it again into the boiling steam. When it was jerked into the air, the stick burst out in flame. It was used to light a walking stick bonfire – "lighted by water".

Photograph by E. C. Kolb

National Geographic Explorer R.F. Griggs Frying Bacon Over a Fumarole.
The steam was so hot and dry as it rushed forth that it was perfectly clear. The pressure lifted the frying pan high in the air. It had to be held down against the outrushing steam.

Photograph by R. F. Grigg

A bonfire kindled by water

"One of the fumaroles was so hot and dry that shavings burst into flame after being plunged for a moment into its hot vapor. Since this consisted of almost pure steam – that is to say, water – a fire was kindled by poking a stick into water." R.F. Griggs, head of the National Geographic Katmai expeditions.

In some of the holes and fumaroles, the steam was dry and the throats of the steam wells red hot. This dry steam at 300 degrees centigrade does not condense until 20 feet up from its source, creating the weird effect of "feather wisps dancing on nothing."

In the hottest of their built-in stove holes, the scientists and part-time cooks fried bacon and baked beautiful golden loaves of bread. A cup of ice-cold glacier water was poured shoulder high into a vent so hot that the water vaporized and disappeared before it reached the ground. Hats thrown into this dry steam jet went sailing thirty feet into the air. At one campsite the frying pan had to be put on a long stick and held down to keep it from wobbling under the pressure. One scientists amused himself by pushing the frying pan into the blower so he could watch the crisp bacon sail through the air. Hungry colleagues caught their athletic breakfast on the fly.

If the housewife is not impressed with cooking facilities in the "Valley of Ten Thousand Smokes", she might be interested in some of the other conveniences such as radial floor heating or a steam-heated tent. At 2300 feet altitude and a few feet in front of a glacial snowbank, the air had a decided chill at night, yet the expedition members had to put most of their bedding under them to keep out the heat. The blankets underneath soon became as hot as the ground. All night long the campers turned and tossed, trying to keep an average sleeping temperature without freezing on the top and roasting on the bottom. Their beds were also damp from the condensation of invisible vapors seeping up through the soil.

Nothing ever dried out completely, and it was thought everyone would catch his death of cold, yet no one did, nor did any of the usual rheumatic pains develop that are common to aging scientists on Arctic field trips. Like the Romans at ancient Stabia and Baia, the temporary inhabitants of "The Valley of Ten Thousand Smokes" found themselves a healthy lot because of the hot thermal waters and not in spite of them.

When it rained, clothes brought dripping wet into the tent were soon merely damp, just like everything else. Once used to this moisture, it was not uncomfortable for the men, but scientific instruments had to be kept on stilts to keep them away from the swelling ground steam.

In his spare time, one of the volcanologists on the expedition amused himself by painting with the multi-colored muds found around the fumaroles.

The fumaroles all emitted at least 98 percent pure steam, but the deposits of other chemicals left on the ground or evaporated out of the steam were valuable, numerous and smelly. In one deposit left by the condensing steam, there was seven percent fluorine, the highest percentage reported anywhere up to that time. Ammonia was found in sal-ammoniac chloride as white and pure as when bought in a drug store.

Crystal "sulphur flowers" lined the throats of many fumaroles, but the sulphuric acid which ate clothes off the line 1500 miles away after Katmai's eruption was uncommon in "The Valley of Ten Thousand Smokes" five years later. Another salt found in the smokes was deadly arsenic, which analyzed 19 percent pure in "King Yellow" deposits. Mixed gasses from the many fumaroles smelled like "rotten eggs" mixed with raw burning wool and the musty odor of a long-lived-in foxhole. If the view in "The Valley of Ten Thousand Smokes" was spellbinding, the odor of the place was anything but hypnotic.

The phenomena of "Ten Thousand Smokes" was caused by the accumulated gas seepings from a great pan of molten lava pushed so close to the earth's surface that it escaped like "the small leaks breaking out of cracks in an old-fashioned bicycle tire from a single puncture in the inner layer of rubber".

Great fissures crossed the edges of the valley like crevasses in a glacier. They were chasms ten feet wide and bottomless. In some of these the steam roared out of underground caverns with a low, hissing sound. It was from these fissures, or from the pressure dome in the center of the valley, that the fumaroles erupted.

One large fissure had a lake in its bottom with a snowbank at one end. Tiny icebergs floated in water which was warm. In another spot a river with water only 15 degrees above freezing raced along sealed fumaroles without warming up, yet the soil on its banks was over the boiling point. There was no consistent pattern, however. At other places, streams quickly evaporated when they hit the steaming fumaroles and the rainy season had no effect on the amount of steam except that moist air condensed over many fumaroles otherwise invisible hot gasses. In this odd place one could see more smokes on a cloudy day than on a day full of sunshine.

The largest of the ten times ten thousand smokes was Novarupta, a crater eight-tenths of a mile across and the only place in the valley where the underlying magma came through the surface to be observed. The crater is atop a dome of its own making, 800 feet across and 200 feet high. It is formed of stiff lava pushed up through the vent, breaking up in huge blocks weighing tons, yet so precariously balanced that they rock back and forth underfoot.

Each group of smokes was different and a more wonderful spectacle than the whole seen in panorama. The desolate valley appeared to be on another planet in the process of formation. To one scientist it was "the devil's own private corner in hell", and to another, "a magnificent circus so big he could not concentrate on any one thing". D.B. Church, the National Geographic group's photographer, tried to capture in words some of the magic he could not get on film as he described the valley:

"A maze of pearly columns that billowed skyward and bent before the strong westerly wind. I started for the nearest fumarole, a short distance away, but it turned out to be half a mile. It was one of the smaller fumaroles, so I crept cautiously up to its edge. From its red-panted throat, which vanished in deep blackness, the sulphur-reeking steam roared forth in a smothering blast."

But the most eloquent description of "The Valley of Ten Thousand Smokes" in its glory comes from the expedition's guide, Walter Metrokin, the one-armed bear hunter of Kodiak. Says Walter, "Smokes all chuck full of valley… Lots of steam… Hell of a place!"

In September, 1918 President Wilson set aside 2,697,590 acres embracing "The Valley of Ten Thousand Smokes", Katmai Volcano, and adjoining scenic wonders as a national park. For many years it was a laboratory for volcanic scientists throughout the world, but by 1935 "Ten Thousand Smokes" had dwindled to ten, and today there are no smokes at all. Wildlife still shies from the desolate, treeless valley, but volcanic activity on the Alaskan Peninsula has shifted elsewhere on the 600 mile rift of active volcanoes which marks the area's unrest.

The famous Father Hubbard, Alaskan explorer and "Glacier Priest," is the only man who has climbed Katmai to look into its crater in both summer and winter. In 1935 he returned to the rim to report its changes. Katmai was then and is now dormant. Not a sign of smoke or life comes from its deepest of all open holes. Inside there are glaciers crawling down its throat. In summer there are scores of waterfalls, all higher than Yosemite, sending their melted ice thousands of feet down the inside walls of the crater. The volcano now echoes the collected roar of water and not the steam and fire of gas and lava. Falling rocks, glaciers, snow and water – Nature is using all her erosion tools to complete the cycle and make Katmai what it was before June 6, 1912 – a frozen, forgotten volcano packed with ice.

Katmai sleeps, but its neighbor, Trident, erupted in 1953, spreading ash over 15,000 square miles.

CHAPTER X

AN EYEWITNESS SPEAKS OUT ON VESUVIUS 79 A.D. THAT DESTROYED POMPEII

The Fiery Letters of Gaius Plinius (Pliny the Younger)

The only eyewitness account of Vesuvius' first eruption in 79 A.D. that has survived the centuries is in the form of two letters sent to Caesar's historian, Tacitus, by 17 year old "Pliny the Younger" after his famous uncle, "Pliny the Elder," a Roman admiral, naturalist and scholar who was killed at Stabiea, one of three cities (Stabiea, Pompeii and Herculaneum) devastated by the catastrophe. Young Pliny, himself later to become a famous Roman lawyer and statesman under Trajan, observed the eruption from 17 miles across Naples Bay at Baia, where he was stationed at the naval base called Misenum.

(LETTER 1)

"Gaius Plinius sends to his friend Tacitus greeting.

You ask me to write you an account of my uncle's death, that posterity may possess an accurate version of the event in your history…

He was at Misenum, and was in command of the fleet there. It was at one o'clock in the afternoon of the 24th of August that my mother called his attention to a cloud of unusual appearance and size. He had been enjoying the sun and, after a bath, had just taken his lunch and was lying down to read; but he immediately called for his sandals and went out to an eminence from which this phenomenon could be observed. A cloud was rising from one of the hills (it was not clear then which one, as the observers were looking from a distance, but it proved to be Vesuvius) which took the likeness of a stone-pine very nearly. It imitated the lofty trunk and the spreading branches, as I suppose, the smoke had been swept rapidly upward by a recent breeze, and was then left hanging unsupported, or else it spread out laterally by its own weight, and grew thinner. It ashes, dirty and streaked. The thing seemed to the philosopher of importance, and worthy of nearer investigation. He ordered a light boat to be got ready, and asked me to accompany him if I wished; but I answered that I would rather work over my books. In fact, he had himself given me something to write.

He was going out himself, however, when he received a note from Rectina, wife of Caesius Bassus, living in a villa on the other side of the bay, who was in deadly terror about the approaching danger, and begged him to rescue her, as she had no means of flight by ship. This converted his plan of observation into a more serious purpose. He got his men-of-war under way, and embarked to help Rectina, as well as other endangered persons, who were many, for the shore was a favorite resort on account of its beauty. He steered directly for the dangerous spot whence others were flying, watching it so fearlessly as to be able to dictate a description and take notes of all the movements and appearances of this catastrophe as he observed them.

Ashes began to fall on his ships, thicker and hotter as they approached land. Cinders and pumice, and also black fragments of rock cracked by heat, fell around them. The sea suddenly shoaled, and the shores were obstructed by masses from the mountain. He hesitated a while and thought of going back again; but finally gave the word to the reluctant helmsman to go on, saying: 'Fortune favors the brave. Let us find Pomponianus.' Pompanianus was at Stabiae, separated by the intervening bay (the sea comes in here gradually in a long inlet with curving shores) and although the peril was not near, yet as it was in full view, and as the eruption increased, seemed to be approaching, he had packed up his things and gone aboard his ships ready for flight, which was prevented, however, by a contrary wind.

My uncle, for whom the wind was most favorable, arrived, and did his best to remove their terrors. He embraced the frightened Pompanianus and encouraged him. To keep up their spirits by a show of unconcern, he had a bath; and afterward dined, with real, or what was perhaps heroic, assumed cheerfulness. But, meanwhile, there began to break out from Vesuvius, in many spots, high and wide-shooting flames, whose brilliancy was heightened by the darkness of approaching night. My uncle reassured them by asserting that these were burning farm houses which had caught fire after being deserted by the peasants. Then he turned in to sleep, and slept, indeed, the most genuine slumbers; for his breathing, which was always heavy and noisy, from the full habit of his body, was heard by all who passed his chamber. But before long the floor of the court on which his chamber opened became so covered with ashes and pumice that if he had lingered in the room he could not have got out at all. So the servants woke him, and he came out and joined Pomponianus and others who were watching. They consulted together as to what they should do next. Should they stay in the house or go out of doors? The house was tottering with frequent and heavy shocks of earthquake, and seemed to go to and fro as if moved from its foundations, but in the open air there were dangers of falling pumice stones, though, to be sure, they were light and porous. On the whole, to go out seemed the least of two evils. With my uncle it was a comparison of arguments that decided; with the others it was a choice of terrors. So they tied pillows on their heads, by way of defense against falling debris, and sallied out.

It was dawn elsewhere; but with them it was a blacker and denser night than they had ever seen, although torches and various lights made it less dreadful. They decided to take to the shore and see if the sea would allow them to embark; but it appeared as wild and appalling as ever. My uncle lay down on a rug. He asked twice for water, and drank it. Then, as a flame with a forerunning sulphurous vapor drove off the others, the servants roused him up. Leaning on two slaves, he rose to his feet, but immediately fell back, as I understand, choked by the thick vapors, and this the more easily that the chest was naturally weak, narrow, and generally inflated. When day came (I mean the third after the last he ever saw) they found his body perfect and uninjured, and covered just as he had been overtaken. He seemed by his attitude to be rather asleep than dead.

In the meantime, my mother and I at Misenum – but this has nothing to do with my story. You ask for nothing but the account of his death…"

(LETTER 2)

"Gaius Plinius sends to his friend Tacitus greetings.

You say that you are induced by the letter I wrote to you, when you asked about my uncle's death, to desire to know how I, who was left at Misnum, bore the terrors and disasters of that night, for I had just entered on that subject and broke it off. Although my soul shudders at the memory, I will begin.

My uncle started off, and I devoted myself to my literary task, for which I had remained behind. Then followed my bath, dinner, and sleep, though this was short and disturbed. There had been already for many days a tremor of the earth, less appalling, however, in that this is usual in Campania. But that night it was so strong that things seemed not merely to be shaken, but positively upset. My mother rushed into my bedroom. I was just getting up to wake her if she were asleep. We sat down in the little yard which was between our house and the sea. I do not know whether to call it courage or foolhardiness (I was only seventeen), but I sent for a volume of Livy, and quite at my ease, read it, and even made extracts, as I had already begun to do. And now a friend of my uncle's, recently arrived from Spain, appeared, who, finding us sitting there and me reading, scolded us, my mother for her patience, and me for my carelessness of danger. Nonetheless, industriously I read my book.

It was now seven o'clock, but the light was still faint and doubtful. The surrounding buildings had been badly shaken, and though were in an open spot, the space was so small that the danger of a catastrophe from falling walls was great and certain. Not till then did we make up our minds to go from the town. A frightened crowd went away with us, and as, in all panics, everybody thinks his neighbors' ideas more prudent than his own, so we were pushed and squeezed in our departure by a great mob of imitators.

When we were free of the buildings, we stopped. There we saw many wonders and endured many terrors. The vehicles we had ordered to be brought out kept running backward and forward, though on level ground, and even when scotched with stones they would not keep still. Besides this, we saw the sea succeed down and, as it were, driven back by the earthquake. There can be no doubt that the shore had advanced on the sea, and many marine animals were left high and dry. On the other side was a dark and dreadful cloud, which was broken by zigzags and rapidly vibrating flashes of fire, and yawning showed long shapes of flame. These were like lightnings, only of greater extent. Then our friend from Spain attacked us more vigorously and earnestly. 'If your brother, your uncle,' and he, 'is alive, he wishes you to be safe; if not, he certainly would wish you to survive him. Why, then, do you delay your flight?' We said we could not bring ourselves to think of our safety while doubtful of his. So, without more delay, the Spaniard rushed off, taking himself out of harm's way as fast as his legs would carry him.

Pretty soon the cloud began to descend over the earth and cover the sea. It enfolded Capeae, and hid also the promontory of Misenum. Then my mother began to beg and beseech me to fly as I could. I was young, she said, and she was old, and too heavy to run, and would not mind dying if she was not the cause of my death. I said, however, I would not be saved without her. I clasped her hand and forced her to go, step by step, with me. She slowly obeyed, reproaching herself bitterly for delaying me.

Ashes now fell, yet still in small amount. I looked back. A thick mist was close at our heels, which followed us, spreading out over the country like an inundation. 'Let us turn out of the road,' said I, 'while we can see, and not get trodden down in the darkness by the crowds who are following, if we fall in their path.' Hardly had we sat down when night was over us – not such a night as when there is no moon and clouds over the sky, but such darkness as one finds in close-shut rooms. One heard the screams of women, the fretting cries of babes, the shouts of men. Some called their parents, and some their children, and some their spouses, seeking to recognize them by their voices. Some lamented their own fate, others the fate of their friends. Some were praying for death, simply for fear of death. Many a man raised his hands in prayer to the gods; but more imagined that the last eternal night of creation had come and there were gods no more. There were some who increased our real dangers by fictitious terrors. Some said that part of Misenum had sunk, and that another part was on fire. They lied; but they found believers.

Little by little it grew light again. We did not think it the light of day, but a proof that the fire was coming nearer. It was indeed fire, but it stopped afar off; and then there was darkness again, and again a rain of ashes, abundant and heavy, and again we rose and shook them off, else we had been covered and even crushed by the weight. I might boast of the fact that not a groan or a cowardly word fell from me in all the dreadful peril, if I had not believed that the world and I were coming to an end together. This belief was a wretched and yet a mighty comfort in this mortal struggle. At last the murky vapor rolled away in disappearing smoke or fog. Soon the real daylight appeared; the sun shone out,

of a lurid hue, to be sure, as an eclipse. The whole world which met our frightened eyes
was transformed. It was covered with ashes white as snow.

We went back to Misenum and refreshed our weary bodies and passed a night
between hope and fear; but fear had the upper hand. The trembling of the earth
continued, and many, crazed by their anxiety, made ludicrously exaggerated predictions
of disaster to themselves and others. Yet even then, though we had been through such
peril and we were still surrounded by it, we had no thought of going away till we had
news of my uncle..."

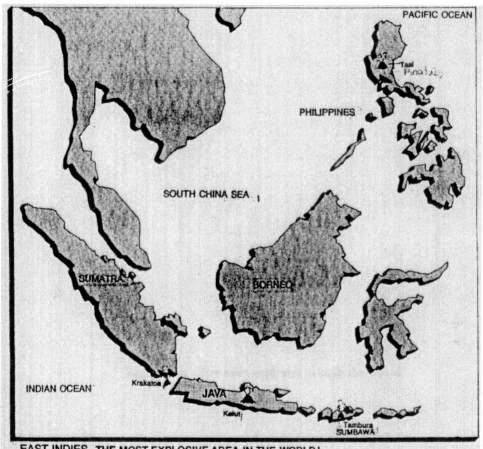

EAST INDIES THE MOST EXPLOSIVE AREA IN THE WORLD!

CHAPTER XI

PINATUBO'S GREATEST IMPORTANCE TO THE U.S. WAS ITS TIMING AND THE BILLIONS OF DOLLARS IT SHOULD SAVE US

At this writing, the ash and chemicals from Pinatubo have resettled back down to earth, reducing the hole in the ozone that it doubled when erupting (a hole already greatly enlarged by El Chichõn, 10 years previous to Pinatubo). There will be other eruptions. A great many soon, and of awesome size between 1980 and 2015 in the turn of the century eruption cycle. None will or could ever come at a more opportune time to save the U.S. from bankrupting ourselves with worthless curbs on our air conditioning, transportation and industry.

Pinatubo put to rest the pseudo scientific theories and misbegotten conception that man made chemicals and man have the ultimate control over global environment as far as strato loading is concerned. This eruption is interesting not because it was one of the world's most horrendous explosions, it wasn't, but because of the vast quantities of gasses and other debris that was thrown high in the sky to load our stratosphere. The following account by an American serviceman brings it close to hand.

PINATUBO UP CLOSE
Eyewitness Account by Lt. Cmdr. William R. Dawson (USN)

By design, my two year tour in the Philippines was supposed to be an education. As a young Navy Lieutenant, there were a great many things about the Navy that I had yet to learn. For that matter, there were a great many things about life that I had yet to learn. A tour at Subic Bay Naval Supply Depot in the Philippines was an ideal opportunity for me to "get up to speed" and learn the inner workings of the complex logistics chain which keeps ships at sea for months at a time. And learn I did... a little operation called Desert Storm gave me a trial by fire. Numerous incidents at home in the Philippines kept me busy as well: Coup attempts in Manila, political assassinations, typhoons, earthquakes, communist insurgents… the Philippines is a country which has its fair share of problems. However, the mother of all calamities came at the end of my tour in Subic Bay, with the horrendous eruption of Mount Pinatubo which had been dormant for 600 years.

The draw-down after Desert Storm was as busy a time in Subic Bay as the actual war itself. Port loading was at its highest level since the Vietnam War. Because the war ended so quickly, vast quantities of material continued to flow into the Supply Center well after the fighting had actually ended. The Depot was literally bursting at the seams. Ships returning from the Gulf continued to require food, fuel, and spare parts, not to mention a well deserved breather before finishing the return trip to the States. Subic Bay had always been considered an ideal liberty port. Offering a large protected deep water harbour and a first rate shipyard, Subic Bay also had quite a well deserved reputation for the large number of bars and massage parlors located in the town of Olongopo across a small bridge from the base. In fact, sailors and marines preferred Subic over Hong Kong, Hawaii, and other West Pacific liberty ports. Whatever you needed, you could find it in Subic Bay. The beer was ice cold, the women friendly, and the shops crowded with inexpensive gifts and souvenirs. My job included having to see to it that visiting ships had all the provisions and supplies they needed prior to leaving port again. As busy as I was with all the ships, I had little time to see my wife, Vicky, much less enjoy the once tranquil lifestyle of the Philippines. No one had any idea of the natural fury which was about to be unleashed.

Sitting only 20 nautical miles from Subic Bay, Mt. Pinatubo was almost in our back yard. In fact, you could see it from the front door of our government-provided, cinder-block duplex. I had never heard of this Filipino volcano until the Stars and Stripes newspaper carried a story one day in late May about how a long dormant volcano seemed to be stirring awake. Earlier in the month some local farmers who kept their livestock on the slopes of the volcano began to spread rumors about how "smoke" was coming out of rocks on the mountain. Everyone dismissed these farmer's stories and continued with their lives. Few others knew the name of the peak on the horizon, much less remembered that Mt. Pinatubo had once been a volcano. Until one day, an European missionary who lived on the slope of the volcano, said that steam was in fact coming out of pores in the hillside and that slight tremors had been felt. At this point Filipino volcanologists as well as a volcano crisis team from the U.S. Geological Survey visited Mt. Pinatubo and confirmed that the volcano was out of its six century sleep.

Volcanic activity began to pick up dramatically in late May. Geological monitors indicated that the slopes of Mount Pinatubo were actually beginning to bulge from the build up of expanding gasses in the magma below the surface. A large "dome" was beginning to form in the crater which indicated to the geologists that a major eruption was in the making. As concerns began to build, the decision was made to evacuate all nonessential personnel from Clark Air Force Base, only eight miles from the volcano, literally at the base of the volcano.

Vicky and I had just returned from a well deserved Memorial Day Weekend trip to the Philippine resort island of Boracay. Earlier in May, Vicky had returned home from a visit to a local orphanage to find three burglars in our house. It was the third break-in on our house in a year, though they never had been bold enough to enter our home in broad daylight before. Vicky was knocked over and shaken as the thieves fled our house and disappeared through the thick jungle that was our backyard. While the naval base had a tall fence with guards, the fence was easily cut and our house was the closest to the jungle. The trip to Boracay was a restful break away from the memories of the break-in and a pause from the hectic pace I had kept during Desert Storm. Although we did not know it yet, Vicky was pregnant with our first child.

After returning from Boracay we went to a Sunday night party at the Officer's Club where word was passed of the decision to evacuate Clark. At the time, we were sure it was only a bad joke or a cruel rumor. Up to that moment, I don't think anyone in Subic really took the threat of the volcano very seriously. The Philippine press had a tendency to blow things terribly out of proportion. They were always very melodramatic, making soap opera drama out of every day life. Surely, this was another mound out of a mole hill. However, Monday morning was an eye opener as 6000 cars, buses, trucks and assorted other vehicles began to stream on to our base from Clark. Leaving my office for an early morning meeting I was struck by the sight of the first arriving cars: 15,000 people were given less than 12 hours to pack one bag per person and leave all their other possessions behind. I have never seen such a sad sight in my entire life. It was truly heart wrenching as I witnessed these first cars of the convoy stream onto our base.

To the Air Force's credit, they handled the evacuation calmly and professionally. As carloads of families funneled out of Clark, they were issued food and personal care items from the PX stores. If the volcano blew, all would be lost anyway, so better that refugees took some stuff with them. This one long caravan snaked its way from Clark through the mountains to Subic Bay. All 15,000 people were "processed" through our gym for the evacuation. Vic called in to the processing center Monday morning to "adopt" one of the families, and at nine that night a young Air Force Lieutenant and his wife, eighteen month old son, and golden retriever came knocking at our door. They were a fun couple, a joy to have in the house. There were lots of horror stories from folks who had close kin of the Adams Family show up at their door step. Unfortunately, or fortunately for them, after two days our first family was able to get aboard a flight heading back to the States. Being the gullible good citizens that we are, Vic and I decided to do our part again and bring in another family as there were still people camping out in their cars and in tents on the base football field. We weren't quite so lucky this time around. Vic came home with two enlisted couples with the world's worst problems on their hands. Neither couple had visas for their partner. As it turned out, one couple was not even married, which meant the U.S. government would not pay for her evacuation. The very cute, seven year old daughter the unmarried couple had in tow was really scared by the traumatic events and wet her bed, poor thing. Or should I say, wet our couch. To make matters worse, the two Filipinas sat on their duffs most of the day, expecting things to be done for them. They became known as the "Clark Kurds" or simply the "House Guests from Hell." As one of our neighbors so aptly put it, "Hospitality is one thing, but this is no time for house guests." To make matters worse, they seemed in no hurry to leave, as the women were afraid of being left behind. An Air Force Chaplain was caught one day performing unauthorized marriages unsanctioned by either the U.S. or Philippine governments. This was not a practice highly regarded by U.S. authorities as they had enough trouble on their hands without having to try to process last minute marriage licenses for what were mostly bar girls looking for a way to get into the States.

I was pretty well tied up at this point trying to help feed all the people Subic had absorbed, while also provisioning the ships still returning from the Gulf. In my position, I supervised all the provisions warehouses on the base. During the war, we had handled all the provisions for Indian Ocean and Persian Gulf naval units. Now we had our hands full keeping all the messes and restaurants on base stocked with fresh food. The onbase population had doubled in the first day of the evacuation. Trying to feed all the hungry mouths was a momentous task.

Another big problem was the lack of pet carriers to evacuate all the dogs and cats from Clark. For sanitary reasons, the order was given to evacuate all animals with families. No one was supposed to have to leave "Fido" or "Mittens" behind in the Philippines. Plane loads of the dog and cat carriers had to be flown in to accommodate the large population of animals on base. Our next door neighbor had the dubious honor of taking in a family with two tiny Chihuahuas. Cruelly, when the family left, they left the dogs behind with our unsuspecting neighbor. Left on their own, the dogs would have quickly died. Our backyard jungle was home to some very large, hungry snakes. What is more, dog meat is considered a delicacy by many Filipino people. Our neighbors kindly adopted the poor creatures.

At this point we were fairly secure in Subic Bay, thinking that the worst we would get would be a light ash dusting. There is a small mountain range between Subic and Clark, so there was virtually no threat of lava flows or mud slides. On Wednesday morning at 9AM there was a large explosion of Mt. Pinatubo which everyone in Subic could plainly see as the weather that day was quite clear. In fact, Vic took a few snapshots from our front yard. A large dark grey and green ash cloud rose very quickly from the direction of the volcano and started mushrooming out in the upper atmosphere. Interestingly, it looked very much like the mushroom cloud from atomic bomb blasts that we all have seen in movies. The exception was that this cloud was in our front yard. Within ten minutes, the cloud was overhead and blocked out the sun. Quite an awesome display, but the winds in the upper atmosphere dispersed the ash cloud before it could settle back to the ground. The cloud was carried out over the China Sea and dumped most of this ash in to the oceans, though some of the ash was carried as far away as Hong Kong. We received no ashfall that day, but San Miguel Naval Station up the road a ways got about half inch of sand-like ash. The feeling of most people was one of curiosity at this point, not fear. There was almost a "block party" atmosphere as people came out of their homes to watch what we thought was the big blow. I remember the Great Blackout in New York City as a child: Everyone had picnics on their front lawns and watched the pitch black Manhattan skyline. The feeling was much the same here as we were sure the ash would not hit us.

However, the explosions did cause panic among the 300,000 people living in Angeles City. Church bells peeled to sound the alarm and many people froze in their tracks. After a few minutes, once they realized the gravity of the situation, people began to race for safety with whatever belongings and livestock they could draw together. There was a tremendous traffic jam as people tried to escape. Just the day before, the city's mayor had stubbornly refused to evacuate the area, claiming fears of the volcano were unfounded. The ash cloud from that day's eruption was clearly seen in Manila, 60 miles away. Scientists predicted that there would be more explosions, as "pyroplastic materials" (a mixture of hot gas, lava, mud and other materials) were seen flowing from the volcano's crater. In fact, volcanologists predicted the volcano could continue to erupt for years. However, prevailing winds would surely carry any volcanic ash away from Subic. After Wednesday, however, we believed the worst was over.

We were wrong. On Saturday the explosions began in earnest. I was at work that day as we had an important supply ship to load and a major storm, Typohoon Yunya, was expected to hit Subic Bay within 24 hours. An earlier typhoon had hit Bangladesh the previous week and we were loading provisions aboard USNS Spica to help relief efforts in that troubled country. Early that Saturday morning, the mountain was rocked by eight explosions that sent huge clouds of ash and steam 19 miles into the sky. The typhoon had enveloped us in dark clouds, buffeting winds and driving rain that morning, so we had no idea the volcano was exploding with such fury until the ash actually began to fall. By chance, the typhoon took a direct westerly path over the volcano and Subic Bay. Storm winds and rain would now bring any ash directly over and down into the Bay. At a little after 8 AM the sky grew very dark and the first traces of ash began to fall on the base.

It began as a light dusting, as if a snow shower. We thought it would blow over in a few minutes, as the previous ash cloud had done. However, things got worse as the sky continued to get darker and darker. The volcano continued to vent its fury, ceaselessly blowing ash over 100,000 feet into the atmosphere. Soon it was totally pitch black outside. The ash clouds completely obliterated all sunlight and the rest of the day was as dark as a moonless night.

Sometimes the ash fell as a fine powder, like fireplace ash. When it fell dry like this, it was tolerable as you could just wipe it off. However, most of the time it came down mixed with heavy rainfall. Mixed with water we really had trouble as it began to stick to everything trees, roads, buildings, people. The grit would clog windshields and cover you in seconds if you walked outside. To make matters worse, the ash-rain mixture had a malodorous sulfur smell and had the consistency of freshly mixed wet cement. Most everyone had been issued a disposable surgical mask to keep from breathing soot. These became valuable commodities and were soon replaced as standard garb by rags and tee shirts tied in front of the mouth and nose. Anything to keep out the suffocating dust.

The dust was bad. However, the darkness was perhaps the strangest and oddest thing about the whole day. In the reduced visibility one of my men was hit by a truck as he walked on a pier. Neither the driver nor the man walking were aware of each other. Fortunately, my worker walked away with only bruises as the truck driver couldn't drive fast with his windshield clogged with ash. At another point in the day, large volcanic rocks the size of golf balls began to fall from the sky. I picked a few up as souvenirs. While large, they were light, very much like pumice stones. I stood in amazement as these stones fell at my feet having been scattered by a violent explosion some 20 miles away. I was glad to have had a hard hat on, but still got a healthy dose of humility as I realized how small and insignificant I was in the grand scheme of things.

Darkness literally engulfed Subic Bay as the base diesel generators had to be shut of due to ash clogging air intakes. Fresh water supplies were also interrupted as the water purification plant could not cope with the amount of ash suspended in river runoff. Poor sewage had prevented the use of Olongopo City water and base water was purified from local fresh water rivers.

The strangest phenomena was the violent lightning and thunder which came with the falling ash. The ash particles were charged from their exploding out of the earth, and as these charge particles fell through the sky they set off tremendous lightning flashes from their static charges. I was to learn later that this violent lightning was normal in ashfalls. At the time, however, it was the most bizarre thing I had ever seen. The flashes came almost ceaselessly and continued virtually all day and on to Sunday morning. I was amazed to learn that no one had been killed by the lightning. I had never seen such sustained, concentrated lightning activity. And in such vivid colors – reds, blue, green and white lightning. Some came in bolts, some in sheets. The thunder boomed, the vibrations felt in your chest. The cracks of lightning and the static electricity set the hair on the back of my neck on end on numerous occasions. A few times I could smell the burn in the air from the bolt, with the thunder boom hitting almost before the lightning did. At one point, I had to cross a long stretch of open ground surrounded by 40' metal shipping containers. I felt sure the lightning Gods would focus on me, this tiny human lightning rod. Somehow, I made it across the field unscathed. We continued to load the ship throughout the early afternoon until we lost all power. The gasoline powered cranes we were using had by this time become clogged with ash, their gears and pulleys locked in place.

In the early afternoon, I began to hear what I was sure was automatic gunfire. I heard a constant popping and cracking coming from the jungle, which I thought at first to be Marines fighting off looters coming in through the jungle. It sounded like a violent fire fight in progress; rumors spread quickly. However, I finally realized that it was the sound of branches ripping away from tree trunks. The weight of the sticky ash stripped all the foliage off trees and shrubs, destroying hundreds of thousands of acres of forest. I realized this must have been the fate of the dinosaurs, with nothing left to eat in some great eruption a million years ago. How helpless those great beasts must have been. All in all, there is nothing in life comparable to this to demonstrate how unbelievably violent

Mother Nature can be when aroused. The beautiful jungles which had taken thousands of years to develop were all being smashed in the space of hours.

In addition to dying dinosaurs, I kept having images of Pompeii in ruins.

I had seen National Geographic specials on Pompeii and had toured the site during a port call in Naples. The vision of the huddled bodies of ash-covered victims kept popping into my head during odd moments of the day. I wondered how archaeologists would find me. What was this idiot doing loading a ship during a volcano explosion? Why wasn't he running away like the rest of the poor ash crusted mummies? I wasn't frightened just amused. I also kept thinking about my Uncle Buck who was writing a book on volcanoes. He would have loved to have seen this one blow so he could get some colorful insight into Vulcan's fury.

On top of everything else happening around us, constant earth quakes shook the ground, a result of the displaced energy from the volcanic core. I had never experienced an earth quake, so was still an "unbeliever" as to their violent nature. The first few tremors were mild ones. In fact, I thought they were just heavy trucks rumbling past my building. The women working in my office knew just what they were, however, as the strength of the shocks quickly grew stronger. The mild tremors merely shook the light fixtures and rattled doors. The bigger quakes felt as if a pair of big men in steel toed boots were kicking your chair from behind. The big ones literally hurt your feet if you were standing when they hit. In the first 24 hours, there were over 250 tremors.

Vic and I kept in touch the whole day via frequent phone calls. I wanted to make sure she was OK and after a big tremor, I would pick up the phone, call, and half jokingly ask, "Wow, how's about that one?" As the day went on, the ash accumulation grew to about six inches and road conditions worsened until I realized that I might not be able to make it up the mile long hill in front of our housing complex. As it got worse, I let a few of my men with families out in town go home to make sure all was OK. I didn't realize until too late that I would not make it home that night. The group of officers I was with scurried from warehouse to warehouse trying to find a safe, dry spot to set up a command post. The weight of the wet ash on the roofs of warehouses began to force open cracks in ceilings and water leaked in everywhere. As the ash continued to fall during the night, power lines fell. In addition, the ash clogged power line insulators, causing grounds and short circuits. We retreated to the ship we had been loading (USNS SPICA) to wait out the ash fall.

And fall it did. At around midnight, warehouses and buildings began to collapse from the combined weight of the rain and ash. Aboard the ship, I had dozed off for a few winks and was startled awake by another lieutenant saying that the Supply Center's security trailer had collapsed with people caught inside. We both ran off into the blackness fearing what we would find but hoping to do what could be done. Two Filipino guards were caught in the wreckage, one with a visibly broken leg. The other was shocked and groggy, but just bruised. They had been asleep in the trailer when the roof collapsed. The weight of the roof "imploded" the building, buckling out the sides and driving the roof downward. Fortunately, heavy desks and filing cabinets had help up major sections of the roof and them from being killed.

As the ambulance took the guards to the base hospital, calls came in over the emergency radio saying that the high school gym had collapsed. Another lieutenant, Jack Sweeny and I grabbed shovels, commandeered a truck and drove the half mile through the now eight inch ash to the school. Fortunately it was not the gym which had fallen as hundreds of Clark refugees were bedded down there for the night. However, a side building had caved in with disastrous results. As Jack and I came running up with shovels to try to dig out anyone caught in the rubble, the first Marine on the scene stopped us and said rather grimly that there was no need to hurry. The two children trapped inside died instantly as the roof fell.

At this point, all I could think about was Vicky at home with our flat roofed two story house. After witnessing the destruction at the school, I didn't put a lot of faith in low-bid government contractors. A quick call home at 2AM assured me all was OK. Not wanting to scare her, I did not tell her of the cave-in at the school. I did tell her some warehouses were buckling and advised her to sleep on the first floor in either the bathtub or under our solid hardwood table. I also told her to check the roof for leaks. The floor was wet in one spot, though fortunately, it was just water runoff seeping in from under the door as the ash built up outside. I felt like a jerk. I had been down the hill working all day and should have been home looking after my family. Fortunately, we still didn't know Vicky was pregnant. I was stressed enough as it was. What a night. It was about this time that the earth quakes really began in earnest. As though we didn't already have it bad enough.

Somehow, Sunday morning came. By this time the ashfall had subsided. As the sun came up on Subic Bay, people ventured out of their homes and discovered their new world. A good friend, John McCarthy, described falling asleep Saturday night not knowing if he would be alive to see morning. He had spent a part of Saturday night trying to shovel heavy ash from his roof. The heavy lightning quickly drove him from the roof. He cuddled up in bed holding his five year old son and said "If this is it, so be it." His relief the next morning was as if he had been spared the executioner's axe.

I finally made it home after daybreak and was relieved to find both Vicky and the house still standing. The trip up the hill had been surprisingly easy in my Japanese made pickup. Cars were abandoned alongside the road and massive tree limbs sprawled across the path making quite an obstacle course. Actually, the housing areas fared quite well. Made from concrete cinder blocks, the solid construction held up to the weight and tremors. Sheet metal carports fell on the cars they were built to protect, but house roofs held under the strain. The local Armed Forces radio station advised of the dangers of cave-ins, so everyone spent most of Sunday shoveling heavy, foot deep ash from their roofs. This chore was back-breaking work, as the foot deep, water logged ash was quite heavy. However, the task was an immediate one as no one knew when the next ashfall would occur and tremors still threatened to collapse buildings.

Shoveling ash is an odd job. The landscape looked as if covered in a heavy snowfall. Only this "snow" wasn't going to melt and was there to stay. The tropical midsummer heat and humidity made the job a sweaty one. Dressed in boots and shorts, shoveling one's roof became the favorite form of exercise. In fact, shovels became a rare commodity. One ship in port was able to fashion shovels out of sheet metal and piping. These became hoarded tools in the days ahead as the process of digging out began.

The rest of the base did not fair as well as the housing areas. Over 250 buildings, or three-fourths of the base was destroyed. The Supply Depot alone lost 19 warehouses from cave-ins. Miraculously, only five Americans were killed, three of whom had been out in town. It should have been much worse. Local engineering personnel spent Saturday night ordering the evacuation of unsafe buildings. In one case, a building collapsed just five minutes after being evacuated. On the Monday following the major eruption, the base was deemed unfit for living and the order was given to evacuate all non-essential personnel. While I had earlier received orders to transfer back to the States the next month, I was deemed essential due to my job as "Mr. Food" and had to stay on for another month.

While power was out all over the base, most of our phone lines continued to work. I believe this is because they were buried underground. In fact, Vicky's mom called from New York on Sunday after the explosion and asked if she was ready to be evacuated. Vicky explained that she must be mistaken, only Clark was being evacuated. But no, her mother had just seen the news on CNN. All dependents were to be evacuated. Through all the guerilla's death threats, typhoons, coup attempts and robberies, Vicky had remained very stoic about life in Subic. Through it all she had assured her mom that things weren't that bad and that the press was exaggerating. Now she looked out the window at the devastation and told her mom, yes, things were bad.

The town of Olongopo had taken the ashfall quite hard. Most of the buildings were poorly constructed. In fact, many of the houses were little more than plywood shacks. Saturday night was a long and terrifying experience for these proud Filipinos. As buildings began to crumble, the mayor of Olongopo asked the base commander to allow the town to evacuate on to the base. However, there was no safe place onboard the base for the town people to go. Thousands of families from Clark were still onboard. The onbase motel with 72 rooms was housing a thousand people alone. With naval buildings falling everywhere, the base commander was forced to deny the mayor's request. Most of the town's residents spent the night huddled in the streets as the buildings provided no shelter. At one point, a rumor quickly spread that the earth quakes had triggered a giant tidal wave which would swamp Olongopo. Tidal waves are a common phenomenon following great eruptions, though one never materialized here. Out of fear of such a wave, much of the town fled to the surrounding hills and did not return until days after the earth tremors stopped.

When the first stream of Clark evacuees started to creep into Subic, Vicky had made a trip to the commissary to buy extra provisions for the hungry mouths we had to feed. Never thinking that we would ourselves be adversely affected by the volcano, Vicky had stocked up on frozen food. In the tropical heat, the frozen meats went bad within two days. When it became apparent all would spoil, we had a great barbecue feast with the last of the good meat. After that we were forced to eat whatever we had at hand. Most meals were peanut butter and crackers, though a cold can of soup filled out our menus. To this day, Vicky still cannot eat Progresso Minestrone Soup and is only beginning to regain a taste for peanut butter. We had a lot of MRE's (prepackaged meals for field consumption) at the Supply Depot left over from Desert Storm. However, we didn't have enough to feed all the 15,000 people left onbase three meals a day. The initial supply of MRE's went quickly as quite a bit of hoarding was naturally occurring. Back up supplies were flown in from Okinawa as soon as the runways were cleared of ash. In addition, the commissary was kept open for business in spite of their collapsed roof. Armed Marines were stationed in the lines to prevent looting and panic. The Marines did a fantastic job keeping order in the long lines that formed outside the commissary. I'm not sure a mob scene would have erupted over food. Though at this point, people were so tired, dirty and hungry, seemingly small episodes could have turned into major situations. No chances were taken.

The Chihuahuas next door were left outside during the whole affair. The poor creatures huddled under lawn chairs as the ash fell around them. As pitiful as they looked, I soon came to hate their ceaseless yapping. The 90 degree heat barely eased up at night. We had to keep our windows open in futile attempts to get any available breeze. As our houses were built to be air conditioned, the windows could not open far enough to let in the cooler night air. It was hard enough sleeping in the heat, but the dogs' howling made things worse. One night they were particularly loud. After tossing and turning for what seemed like hours, I finally could take it no longer. I disappeared for five minutes and the barking stopped. When I came back to bed, Vicky asked what I had done. I calmly replied, "I killed them." After numerous sleepless nights due to the heat and chihuahua barking, Vicky could only reply "Oh," and rolled over and quickly fell asleep. Actually, the poor dogs had gotten themselves into such a frenzy that their leashes had become hopelessly tangled and they were pinned under their lawn chairs. As soon as I straightened their leashes the dogs had fallen asleep exhausted.

Another friend had a pet rabbit in Subic, named "Ashley Rabbit." A friendly, indoors sort of rabbit with a bad habit of chasing cats, Ashley liked to scamper about in his relatively safe backyard to get his exercise. One day after the explosion he disappeared. I suspect poor Ashley fell into someone's cooking pot.

We had a few diesel powered 40' refrigerated shipping containers at the Supply Depot which we were able to spread out across the base as needed. The Commissary used a few, as did the Air Station to keep whatever food remained cold. I had the dubious distinction of setting one refrigerated van up at the hospital to act as the base morgue until the hospital could regain power. That is how I came to know the exact number of fatalities from the volcano.

Electrical power took a while to be restored as each electric pole had to be mounted by technicians with brooms and fire hoses. Before power could be restored, all insulated power contacts had to be cleared of the volcanic ash which has a heavy silicon content and high conductive properties. In addition, the individual diesel power units at the power plant had to be cleared of the ash which had clogged their air intakes. My large refrigerated and frozen warehouses had power restored in three days, and they were located only a block from the power plant. The rest of the base took longer. It would be a month before power was restored in our housing areas. The day immediately after the big flow, looters came in through the jungle and cut away the long power cable which ran up the hill to the housing area. Anxious to get the copper in the cable, the thieves dragged a few hundred feet of it back off into the jungle. The cable was sold on the black market for scrap, though I later heard that the Navy was able to get some of it back.

Looting was a problem in the housing areas as well. The villagers in the town of Olongopo were hit hard and had no place to go for food but onto the base. The only problem was, we didn't have any food either.

On the Monday following the eruption, Vicky began the painful task of packing her one bag she was allowed to take with her. This is an exercise every person should do annually as a mental exercise, if for nothing else. Pack just one bag with all the things in life you really care about. What stays and what goes? We never thought we would ever get anything besides what Vicky could carry out of the Philippines. Fortunately we had three days to decide what to bring and what to leave behind. Vicky took a few pieces of clothing, our wedding pictures, some family heirlooms and whatever wedding gifts she could fit in one duffle bag. We also packed three boxes of valuables which I promised to find a way to mail one way or another. I thought that the least I could do was find an Academy classmate on one of the ships in port to take the boxes back to the States with him. I hated to leave these things behind to the looters as had happened at nearby Clark Air Force Base.

Policy was put out that those with only three months remaining on their tour should evacuate with the dependents. I thought at first that Vicky and I would be able to leave Subic together as I had less than a month to complete in my two year tour. However, I was stamped "Essential Personnel" due to the nature of my job. The ships that were headed back from the Gulf diverted to Subic to help evacuate the base. As ships would pull into port to load refugees aboard, we would outfit them with all the food and supplies they needed to feed the hungry mouths they took onboard. A big problem for the ships was the lack of diapers, extra bedding and infant formula: Not items the typical warship carries in her storerooms.

These were less than ideal conditions to say goodbye to Vicky. I had to work long hours loading refugees and food aboard ships. Yet at the same time, I had to get my own life back in shape. Through it all Vicky was a symbol of courage. Every new setback she faced with a smile and a determined attitude. However, the night before she left she finally broke down. We were still having quite violent earthquakes. At night, the tremors would wake you in bed before they actually hit. For some reason, you could sense them moments before they hit and you would stir from a sleep wondering what it was that had disturbed you. Perhaps it was the quietness.

A moment later they would hit. On this night, the quakes were coming hard and often. They would shake the bed and rattle the brass handles on my dresser. The quakes were enough to make you jumpy, but the sound of the brass rattling set us on edge. I was about to tape them shut, when we heard a new rumbling. And then bright lights came in through our window. I looked out to see Marine armored tanks going up the street. Looters had been spotted coming in through the jungle the previous nights and a few shots had even been fired. The tanks were patrolling the housing areas as a deterrent. Deterrent to our sleep, most likely. At the sight of the tanks, Vicky finally had enough. She broke down, and for the first time admitted that she was scared and wanted to go home. Although we were able to get all our household goods back to the States, Vicky refused to let the dresser with the brass handles back in the bedroom. The sound of those rattling handles still evokes vivid memories.

On the Thursday after the explosion, I went with Vicky and our neighbors, the McCarthy's, down to the processing station to begin the evacuation process. Vicky was a low priority as we didn't have any kids, and we still didn't know that Vicky was pregnant. We still didn't have a pet carrier for Vicky's cat, "Scotia," so we put her in a small duffle bag with a crack for her head to poke out. Scotia was a small black Filipina cat with a bent tail. I was sure she would live out her cat days in the Philippines, never to get her "green card," but after all that we had been through, I didn't feel right leaving her behind.

After hours in the processing line, we finally got a ship assignment for Vicky. She would be travelling to the island of Cebu with Lieutenant John McCarthy and I quickly ran down to the ship making it there before our wives' bus. On the Merrill's quarterdeck, I found a classmate from Annapolis, Marcus Yonehiro had the duty. The Merrill turned out to be full. However, with Marcus' help, we were able to convince the Merrill's Captain that he could squeeze a few more onboard. A quick chase ensued as John and I had to commandeer a Jeep and flag down the wives' departing bus. It all happened so quickly, and we had all been so busy, I didn't realize Vicky was gone until later. Aboard ship that night, Vicky had her first shower in a week, a warm meal with ice cream dessert, and a nice bed in an air conditioned space. Though she would not make it back to the States for a week, she was on her way.

I entered a stage where I worked like a dog, relieved that Vicky was safe and homeward bound, and that I would hopefully soon join her. The decision had been made to dig out from under the ash and make Subic Bay like it once was before Mt. Pinatubo exploded. We had a long road ahead of us.

In the coming weeks the volcano continued to spew ash. Fortunately, these were much smaller eruptions, and the ashfall fell mainly to the north. However, one morning, we woke up and found that another ash fallout had come down during the night. While only a small dusting, two weeks after the main explosion, we were still gun-shy of another big blow. The dusting was enough to jolt us back to reality and let us know that Mother Nature was still angry and man could do little or nothing to appease her. These eruptions were more sedate than the first ones. The clouds didn't obscure the sun like the first few, though a few vents of ash put dust clouds high into the atmosphere. Earthquakes continued to be bad. In fact, one particularly bad tremor literally threw me from bed one night. Nothing broken, except my shattered nerves.

After all the rain from my typhoon, the next few weeks were dry. As the sun baked the ash dry, the resulting dust became a constant nuisance. Drying to a fine powder, the dust permeated everything. Thick clouds of this dust would get kicked up by wind blowing over roof tops. Like in a bad snowstorm, visibility would fall to zero in these gusts. Driving a car became a test of nerves as you could barely see the car in front of you. Tail lights were encrusted in ash and became useless. One quickly learned to avoid driving behind large trucks as they tended to obscure everything with their dust clouds. One quick trip outdoors left one thick with grit, and by the end of a workday, most all of us were caked with sweat and dirt. I don't think I ever have been so dirty in my life, Uncle Buck's summer camp included. With apologies to the singer Mary Martin, "I want to wash that ash right out of my hair."

"To you Uncle Buck, and the readers of your volcano book, I know you have written much on Mt. Pinatubo and how it has affected world air pollution so I thought you also might like to know how it felt up close to an American serviceman. As to my Vicky, I am pleased to report that she somehow became pregnant during all this as we were surprised to find out after she arrived home. After things were all cleaned up, I followed her and was next stationed in Jacksonville, Florida. Subic Bay is no longer a U.S. Naval Base."

Steamed Cleaned and Stretched

Dionisio covered a steam vent with his hat and rode his burro into the town of Paricutin to tell the priest. "Keep it under your hat," said the padre, but it was too late, when Dionisio returned, he'd grown a bare headed volcano.

Put a Lid on It Senators

Since Dionisio Pulido proved that man cannot put a lid on a volcano, maybe man will put his lid on something he can control like deficit spending.

CHAPTER XII

PARICUTIN – A FRIENDLY TOURIST VOLCANO
The Mexican Peasant Who Planted Corn and Grew A Volcano

How would you like to grow your own private volcano, a gigantic mountain landfill 2,343 feet high and then have the government take it away? This is about what happened to Dionisio Pulido, a Mexican farmer in 1943.

Dionisio Pulido stood in his own flat cornfield tilling the soil as he had for years. But this was different. The soles of his bare feet were strangely warm, his ears pounded with a continuous, surf-like roar, his body trembled and shook with the earth; fear filled his simple heart, and he ran two miles to his village to spread the word and seek the advice of his priest.

How does it feel to be on top of a volcano when it decides to break out into the open?

According to the account of the one living man who knows, it is not much fun. The survivor of this most spectacular eruption, a Tarascan Indian, was literally on top of Mexico's Paricutin February 20, 1943, when it ruptured the earth's crust and made its first public appearance. Dionisio Pulido looks no different from any of the 500 other Mexicans who inhabited the village of Paricutin before it lost its name to the volcano that buried it.

Guides will tell you this "legal owner" of a volcano he cannot use, is a giant of a man who discovered steam coming out of a hole in the ground and put his hat over it to ward off evil spirits while he went to lunch.

When he returned the hat was on top of a mountain and well steamed. None of the story is quite true. The hat stayed on Dionisio Pulido, and he is not a big man but a little fellow with brown complexion, a mustache and scraggly beard, a perpetual scowl and wide nostrils. Clad in his typical white, smock-like costume and wearing a broad-rimmed straw, it is virtually impossible to pick him out from a group of his fellow citizens.

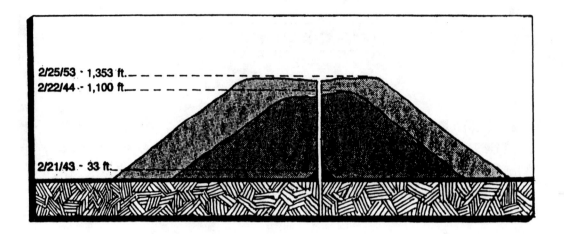

**1,000,000 visitors saw Paricutin grow for 10 years,
the world's friendliest, most studied volcano.**

If Dionisio Pulido is a giant at all it is not because of his size but due to his experience. He is the only living man who was actually on top of a volcano when it burst into throbbing existence.

For some time prior to February, 1943, on a tract of land of Rancho Tepacua in the Mexican state of Michoacan, there was a strange and miraculous hole. The land and its hole were owned by Dionisio Pulido and occasionally his children would amuse themselves by casting dirt and stones into the hole. It never seemed to fill up. Odd sounds like the chuckle of boiling water could be heard whenever Dionisio stopped there to warm his hands over the hot breath coming out of the hole's mouth.

On February 5, 1943, the valley trembled with shock waves for the first time. On each succeeding day the tremors were more violent, the rumblings more thunderous – and when they weren't sleeping or working their fields the Indians were praying. In order to ward off evil spirits they set up a sacred image, El Senor de los Milegros, in the plaza. The statue faced directly toward the property of Dionisio Pulido.

February 20th dawned clear and calm and Dionisio, after a hearty breakfast of frijoles, tacos and tortillas, took his oxen and headed for the cornfield to do some plowing. Although the earth was rippling gently, the thunder was distant and remote. After two weeks Dionisio was used to it, but he had no way of knowing that the embryo was getting impatient and that directly underneath his feet a lava reservoir was working itself into a white-hot frenzy. Around noon his wife, Paula, joined him. Later on a friend by the name of Demetrio Toral pitched in.

Shortly after 4:00 P.M. the eternal rumbling increased in intensity. A fissure snaked across the black, fertile soil. A wisp of steam curled upwards. Cracks appeared. There was a growing roar. The earth shook.

Startled, the three Indians drew back. Trembling Dionisio, uneducated though he was, knew that there was impending danger in the great crack across his field. He ordered his wife and Demetrio to flee to the village, while he thriftily went to retrieve his ox and plow. With each minute the activity increased, smoke issued from the fissures as from an elongated smudge-pot, the heat was intense and the noise was that of a wind-blown forest fire.

At this time there passed one Aurora de Cucura who had seen the commotion from the kitchen door of her adobe farm house. She paused long enough to get a good scare and then fled onward along the road to the village of Paricutin, two miles away.

Before the terrified farmer had finished saving his plow, and unhitching his oxen, the volcano began to blow. As he retreated hastily to the town his field received its most thorough and final plowing. The prologue of rolling tympani and crashing cymbals lasted only two hours, and then, starting at 6:00 P.M., large stones were abruptly catapulted through an abscess in Pulido's dispossessed cornfield. They were like flaming footballs being kicked out onto the valley floor. By 10:00 P.M. the glow from the slowly-rising mountain lit up the valley so brightly that educated villagers could sit outside and read their newspapers, little realizing their humble village would soon be in the headlines.

Suspecting they faced a rather serious problem, the citizens of the town consulted a book on Mt. Vesuvius in the church. Only then did they realize that it was a volcano they had growing among the corn stalks.

The word was flashed to the rest of the world, and almost at once the experts, men of science and government along with an endless stream of curious tourists began their trek to the valley of Cuyiziro and a view of the world's newest volcano.

The genie was out of the bottle, and there was no getting it back in. Twenty-four hours after its birth, the rambunctious newcomer was a noisy, burping baby 30 feet high. White vapors, blue fumes, tongues of flame and searing steam all added to the confusion that had replaced the orderly life on Dionisio's once fertile farm. Throughout the valley hungry cattle ran about bellowing with terror as the corn field exploded its load high over their heads, dropping hot sand on their backs and burying their pasture in ash. The hysterical farm animals and their masters could actually watch a mountain grow.

During the second day (February 21st) a particularly violent earthquake forced the peons to flee their homes, convinced that the world was coming to its end. It was later established that the 'quake,' which originated several hundred miles away in the ocean off Acapulco, was only indirectly connected with the eruption, but you couldn't expect the villagers of Paricutin to believe this even if they had been told.

Consternation gripped the inhabitants as they debated whether to remain and protect their homes or to get out while the getting was good. Fortunately, this was no Mount Pelee inundating a St. Pierre with a jet-propelled glacier of fire and horror. This was more like a slow-motion cinema. In the end the volcano decided the issue – the lava began to flow. There was no stopping the evil mass as it carried all before it. Trees snapped like matchsticks, crops disappeared, and the people fled the valley.

No lives were lost – this was a considerate volcano. Its destruction was limited to non-human things. The nearest thing to human harm occurred much later when an American woman tourist suffered a broken rib when the shed she was standing under collapsed with an overload of ash.

On February 26th, when it was but six days old, Paricutin was a hundred feet high. There were thirty to forty eruptions a minute as the extremely active volcano spewed out a column of smoke and flames that shot 20,000 feet into the atmosphere. Stones shot up 3,500 feet as fiery snowballs rolled down the cone. Ashes rained on every village within 200 miles, including Mexico City. The panicked Tarascans of the doomed valley dug crosses into the ground hoping to halt the inevitable lava flow. Those crosses are now buried under a 50-foot-deep lava lake. The lava, too, was considerate, flowing at a speed of only two yards per hour.

To paraphrase a historical saying: "Paracutin had its messengers of defeat – St. Pierre had none…"

Inexorably the rising tide of lava and the deadly snowfall of ash made the village a ghost town. Dionisio Pulido and his family and all the other families piled into Army-supplied brigade trucks and headed for Parangaricutiro, a rival town, where their former antagonists took them in. Ultimately, Paricutin, the town, was entombed under 13 feet of lava and ashes. Now there is no confusion for the mailman with a letter addressed to Paricutin – he knows the only surviving Paricutin in Mexico is a volcano.

It took nearly a full year for the flood to reach Parangaricutiro, but it, too, was abandoned and shared the same lava tomb as its sister town.

As Paricutin continued to grow it sealed off Dionisio's church and buried it

The lava was not the vicious sticky mass so common to Hawaiian volcanoes. It hardened almost at once and broke off into huge chunks in its own path, live massive furnace clinkers, incandescent and gaseous. At night the performance was even more spectacular with the darkness lighted by colorful pyrotechnic shows that were dazzling to the enthusiastic audience which gathered to watch and even burst into spontaneous applause after a particularly impressive arc of fire.

Paricutin not only had an enthusiastic audience – it had a fan club chronicling its growth and comparing it with long-established volcanoes.

Paricutin showed no signs of shame that it had never killed anybody. It seemed to prefer its role as an actor. The eager youngster added an encore to the display by spitting out chunks of lava in the shapes of birds and fish flying effortlessly through the sky. The natives began to attribute occult powers to these "creatures" believing they actually resided in the crater. More than 2700 tons of material per minute came out, often through abscesses in the sides of the cone. If this had been steel, there would be enough to build 1440 U.S. Navy destroyers per day – or one every minute! The total output was more than the sediment deposited in a year by all the rivers in the world. Dionisio Pulido could not have hauled it away with all the ox carts ever built. It was 500 times the Mississippi's yield of 450,000,000 tons of mud a year.

On an average of every six seconds for several months, "El Monsturo", as the Indians called Paricutin, erupted with the regularity of a Yellowstone geyser.

With such a natural, home-grown attraction, it did not take the peso-minded entrepreneurs long to organize tours. The genie had brought utter and final combustion to the twin villages of Paricutin and Parangaricutiro, but the loud-mouthed giant also brought unparalleled prosperity to the citizens of the two villages. Although Dionisio Pulido technically owned the volcano, he does not receive any royalties for it. The mineral rights under his land will always belong to Vulcan.

In the ten years that Paricutin erupted, more than one million visitors viewed the smoking peak. Guides from the buried cities were in great demand as they led their charges to within 1300 yards of the crater wearing rented clothes and riding rented horses. The guides spin yards about their personal experiences with El Monsturo. The new industry of the area was not only better than farming peso-wise, but telling stories about the volcano was surely easier and more fun than plowing a field, especially when the volcano was a noisy, musical comedy showoff who had never hurt anybody. It was also a geologic pet because witnesses were on hand from its very inception and not a life was lost to its ire. Consequently, it was the most observed and pampered of all volcanoes. For ten years it reciprocated in kind by providing tourists and natives with the greatest free show on earth, obediently blasting tons and tons of hot rocks skyward and lighting up the night with technicolor glows. If Paricutin lacks the destructive courage of its older brothers, the superstitious natives don't want to crowd their luck taking chances even for the Yankee dollar. After all, those stones the volcano so casually tossed out are hot, and the natives can remember at least one death as a prelude to the supernatural eruption. It started with a Hatfield-McCoy type of feud and, scientific explanations to the contrary, most of the Indians still believe Paricutin burst forth as a deadly warning for them to cleanse their sins and change their ways. Some 500 Tarascan Indians lived in the town of Paricutin 180 miles west of Mexico City and a similar distance northwest of the Pacific resort of Acapulco. There was a neighboring village called Parangaricutiro. The nearest city of any size is Urapan with 20,000 souls. Today, with both Paricutin and Parangaricutiro gone, there is nothing between Urupan and the volcano except ashes and lava.

For some years before the eruption buried them, there was a dispute between the two villages over land rentals, a running battle that set brother against brother, with charges and countercharges. Actually, no one took it very seriously, and in fact looked forward to the next altercations until one of the participants was killed. His name was Nicholas Toral.

Following the death of Toral a huge rock and a cross were erected as a kind of peace monument on the spot where he died between the two towns. For a time there was peace. But one day the cross was found chopped down and the superstitious Indians took this as a sign that the gods would be offended. From that day onward they lived in dread of some supernatural retaliation. How right they were!

The spot where Nicholas Toral was killed and his cross chopped down is the very spot in Dionisio's cornfield where Paricutin emerged. It is also in a direct line with the face of the holy statue erected in the plaza to protect the villagers from harm. As a further coincidence, it was a relative and namesake of Nicholas Toral who was the last man to be with Dionisio Pulido just prior to the eruption.

Paricutin, thought to be completely burned out, erupted again in 1952… not a big eruption, but just enough to show the world that even friendly comic opera volcanoes are not to be taken for granted.

James A. Michener

Our deep appreciation to James A. Michener for consenting to let us use
his chapter Volcanic Atoll, which is the process by which islands grow

CHAPTER XIII

THE ATOLL VOLCANIC ISLAND BUILDING
By James Michener

The Atoll, an essay by James Michener is reprinted here by special permission from the author in his early book *Return to Paradise*. It is significant to point out that the atolls (volcanic islands) are responsible for the discovery of North America by the Vikings even as the mini Ice Age about 1000 A.D. sucked water from the North Atlantic and created many islands which had formerly been shoals. A similar phenomena occurred earlier to bring underwater shoals in the Bering Sea above water. While this book specifically points out that the computer model predictions of a global warming trend has not occurred in the last 500 years, evidence does indicate a cooling trend caused by volcano stratosphere loading did and could create such a phenomena again as it did about the year 1000. This is quite the opposite of the coastal flooding predicted by the doomsayers in their faulty global warming evidence.

"…a symbol of all men seeking refuge, the security of home, the warmth and love, lost in a wilderness of ocean, the atoll is a heaven that captivates the mind and rests the human spirit."

James A. Michener

Our deep appreciation to the late James A. Michener for consenting to let us use his chapter volcanic atoll which is the process by which islands grow.

The Atoll by James A. Michener (from *Return to Paradise*) "Ages ago, when the world was different, the South Pacific contained many islands we have never known. Then as now the floor of the ocean rose and fell when volcanic pressures fluctuate. A violent up-thrusting that created new islands would be followed by an imperceptible subsidence which slowly dragged the newborn lands back below the surface of the sea.

About 10,000 years ago one such mountainous island rose above the warm waters near the equator. Around its edges swarmed a multitude of remarkable animals, the coral polyps, taking refuge in deep water. Slowly they began to build a calciferous reef, each new polyp adding his tiny limestone skeleton to those that had died before.

The polyps had chosen their new home with studied care. The water temperature must never go below 68 degrees, or the tiny animals would freeze. The base of their building could be no deeper than 120 feet, or they would drown. The water must be salty, but not too salty, and it had to contain an abundance of plankton, that microscopic marine life on which coral feeds. Most important of all, the water had to be fresh and free of sand, for any kind of sedimentation would suffocate the polyps.

Working slowly, dying by the multiple billions so that their limestone structures could become rock, the polyps clung to the shores of the new island and in some years raised their reef as much as three inches. Of course, the highest point was still far under water and no eye could have discerned that a miracle had already begun to take place.

For now the ever-violent ocean bed began steadily to subside. In a thousand years it fell perhaps three feet, but slowly the island was settling under the sea. Unseen, the coral continued building. Now it was less than fifty feet below the surface.

Then one day the dying island exploded into cataclysmic fury. Its volcanic flames lighted the sky for many years, but as the fierce heat died out the entire ocean bed island, reefs, coral and all – shivered and sank deeper into the sea.

The coral was not drowned. Through many centuries, it continued to build until a final day when, with some unchronicled gasp, the last fragment of the original island disappeared forever.

More than a thousand years elapsed and in that time the coral on the sunken reef continued its patient growth. It was now close to the surface and one day a solitary limestone pinnacle no bigger than a pencil broke the waves. A score of decades passed. A bird skimming the empty wastes of ocean could have seen a thin shining ribbon of white coral. A piece of driftwood caught fast and rotted. Sand began to collect and finally a seed drifted two thousand miles across the waves and found lodgment. A casuarina tree began to grow.

It was washed away. More soil collected. Igneous rock from some recent volcano floated mysteriously to the almost-born island. Sand edged the inner shore of the reef. A coconut arrived, a pandanus. In two thousand years a new fragment of earth had been created.

Now the entire reef, miles in circumference, threatened to break the surface. Within the circle the sea water became dirty and all polyps on the inner shore died. Those on the outside now did the work, building the reef ever outward from its center.

A new violence, a new upheaval of the ocean floor and the entire reef was lifted twenty feet into the air. Here and there weak portions crumbled into the pounding sea, leaving narrow channels into the lagoon. At other points, where coral skeletons had been piled highest, substantial islands rose like a cluster of jewels strung along the golden strands of the reef.

At last the miracle was complete! A coral atoll, circular in form, subtended a shallow lagoon. On the outer edge giant green combers of the Pacific thundered in majestic fury. Inside, the water was blue and calm. Along the shore of the lagoon palm trees bent their towering heads as the wind directed, and after a thousand more years brown men in frail canoes came to the atoll and decided it should be their home.

The world contains certain patterns of beauty that impress the mind forever. They might be termed the sovereign sights and most men will agree as to what they are: the Pyramids at dawn, the Grand Tetons at dusk, a Rembrandt self-portrait, the arctic wastes. The list need not be long, but to be inclusive it must contain a coral atoll with its placid lagoon, the terrifyingly brilliant sands and the outer reef shooting great spires of spindrift a hundred feet into the air. Such a sight is one of the incomparable visual images of the world.

This is the wonder of an atoll, that you are safe within the lagoon while outside the tempest rages. The atoll becomes a symbol of all men seeking refuge, the security of home, the warmth of love. Lost in a wilderness of ocean, the atoll is a haven that captivates the mind and rests the human spirit.

More than a symbol, however, the atoll is a reservoir of tangible beauty. Fleecy clouds hang over it, so that in the dawn it wears a flaming crest of gold. At midday it seems to dream in the baking heat, its colors uncompromisingly brilliant. At sunset the clouds once more reflect a shimmering brilliance. At night stars seem to hover just out of reach, and if there is a moon it does not dance upon the waters. Its reflection lies there passively like a silvered causeway to the opposite shore.

Each of the motus along the reef – the independent islands with trees – has its own characteristic charm. Some have beaches a mile wide of such dazzling sand as to blind the unprotected eye. Others contain coral gardens that delight the imagination. Still others are the home of a thousand birds, the prowling ground of sharks, the keepers of the caverns where pearls grow.

The coral itself is infinitely colored. Most startling are the bright, untempered hues: radiant blacks, garish greens, bright blues, enviable yellows and brooding purples. But after the shock of seeing such prodigal brilliance, it is the pastels that continue to invite the eye. There are delicate pinks, soft blues and airy greens. Sometimes a single patch of coral will contain a dozen shades. Again there will be an acre of one primitive color alone. Only on a living reef can you see the pageantry of coral, for once dead and exposed to air, its color fades and vanishes.

Also infinite are the forms of coral. Most spectacular are the branching arms that seem to clutch outward toward the ocean. Most unforgettable is the brain coral which reproduces in arresting likeness the shape and convolutions of the human brain. There are shelves of coral, trees of coral, great gloves of it, angular skeletons, and even delicate flowers. Each is composed of the dead remnants of millions of polyps.

But to savor the true miracle of coral, you must go to the outer edge of the reef. There, suspended by ropes from a small boat, you push yourself down, down along the living face of the majestic structure. Whereas the lagoon waters were delicate and sprinkled with sunlight, the brooding waters at the reef face are sullen and black. Below you, as far as the eye can penetrate, there is nothing but great chunks of mysterious forms jutting into the breaking sea. Sometimes the reef has broken away and left small caverns. Your hand explores one and draws back in terror. An octopus hides there. Then your eye becomes accustomed to the mournful darkness and you see about your face a myriad of brilliant fish. You look in amazement, for never have you ever guessed such creatures could exist. In every possible form and color these astonishing fish drift by. When you think you have seen all the wonders a reef can hold, a monstrous coral fish goes past. It has a dozen silky tails, streamers from each fin, a face like a pig's, a striped body like a zebra's and such colors as no artist would ever combine. Off into the caverns it goes, and your eye lingers on a dark shape gliding through the mysterious waters. Was it a shark? It turns on its side and disappears. And always at your elbow the fantastic shapes of coral, the brilliant colors, the provocative textures. Above you the great surf pounds, and now your lungs throw with pain. You pull upon the rope and lunge toward the surface, up past the glorious fish, the murky caverns and the living coral. You break the waves and catch a comber full in the face. Exhausted, you climb back into the boat. You have seen the face of the reef, the battleground from which the atoll rose, and you will never forget what you have seen.

This is how an atoll looks. Along the outer edge toward the sea – nothing. A few trees perhaps, a stretch of blinding sand, some bird nests. Along the inner shore of the largest motu a string of thatched huts, each with its share of beach. Next, three or four shacks built of wood and corrugated iron. Then a trading store with a veranda for the loafers. Then a European house painted white and red, the government quarters. Finally a big church, whitewashed, with sloping roof leading to three huge concrete tanks, also whitewashed. These are for the collection of rain, since no atoll has enough fresh water for cooking and drinking.

And everywhere there are coconut palms. This amazing tree is the life blood of the atoll. Its wood makes furniture. Its plaited leaves makes fine baskets or hats or carpeting or partitions. A silky lace-like growth about the crown yields good mats. The heart of the palm makes the world's best salad, the husk is perfect insulating material, and the hard shell of the nut makes good charcoal.

As if this were not enough, the liquid within the nut is a delicious substitute for drinking water and is moreover so pure that it can be used medically as a completely sterile saline solution. With safety it can be injected even into the blood stream, for in the hard shell there is always a soft eye through which a needle can be passed.

As for the meat itself, its uses are manifold. Few nuts are allowed to ripen into the hard, unpalatable stuff sold in American markets. If they do reach that age, when the milk is bitter and useless, they are made into copra for their oil, which is manufactured into soap and margarine. Most nuts are picked young, when the meat is so soft that it can be eaten with a spoon. There are six stages in the ripening of a coconut, each with its peculiar cooking possibilities.

The best dish is this: Take a fish caught that afternoon on the reef and cut it into strips, raw. Soak them overnight in lime juice and sea water. Pick some young coconuts and add their milk to the fish. Stand the pot in the sun for five hours. Grate up the coconut meat, add two onions and mix it with the fish. Add some salt. The result is a kind of bittersweet dish which tastes completely different from any other food. There is no smell of fish, no taste of sea water, no bite of lime. It is a delicious feast.

But more than the beauty, more than the coral, more than the subtle food, it is the native people who make an atoll so strange and yet so attractive. By some curious chance the natives on most Pacific atolls are Polynesians. These brown navigators consistently bypassed the commodious islands like New Guinea or the Solomons to seek out tiny atolls. Along the north coast of New Guinea there are many specks in the ocean populated by Polynesians. And scattered through the Solomons there are others. But to see atoll life at its best you must go farther east beyond Tahiti, where there are so many low-lying islands that they seem to form clouds along the horizon. There Polynesians have built a true island culture...

The atolls are beautiful. They are among the most beautiful features on this earth, and it is no wonder they have lured many men. Not even the wild hurricanes, the loneliness, the stinging flies or the bitterness of a life slipped past can subtract one portion of the crystal beauty of these miraculous circles in the sea. In spite of all the men who have died of atoll fever, the lagoon and the pounding surf are incomparably wonderful.

Much romantic nonsense has been written about the atolls. Even the word lagoon has been debased far below its true currency. On the motus the beautiful girls have been ridiculed; the patient native men have been burlesqued. A thousand wastrels have befouled the islands; a hundred sentimentalists have defamed them.

But there still remains this fact: when the great seas pound upon the reef, when the stars shine down upon the lagoon, there is a mysterious, fragile something that no amount of misrepresentation can destroy. To say that men have died in such places, engulfed in disillusion and despair, is merely to point out that on a lonely atoll, as in most cities, good men find loveliness, weak men find evil."

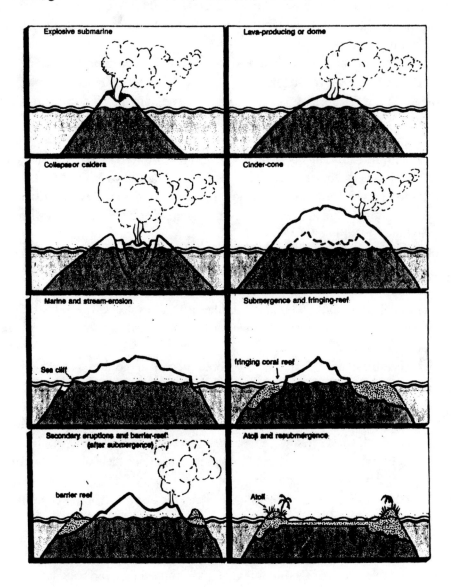

A volcanic island grows and changes with eruption, erosion and coral growth.

VOLCANO SHORTIES

Ngorongora Stew

Ngorongora is a flat-bottomed volcano crater 13 miles across and 2000 feet deep, with majestic waterfalls feeding a lake surrounded by a thick blanket of clover on which sleep 75,000 wild animals that eat the clover and each other.

On hearing about his natural stockyard of hyenas, lions, hippopotamuses, zebras, cheetahs, rhinoceroses, jackals, baboons, and even ostriches, the Kaiser is supposed to have planned a meat canning factory near the volcano. Soon afterwards, he lost his lease on East Africa but his aborted plan raises all sorts of speculation. Perhaps he hoped to feed the whole German army by filling the crater with water and then goading the volcano into boiling up a great stew. There has never been a volcano which erupted rhinoceros steaks, but this is about the only thing volcanoes have not done although neither the Kaiser nor the current U.S. politicians have the slightest effect on what a volcano might do.

Tin Can Island

Perhaps the most unusual of the South Sea islands is Niuafou, northernmost of the "Friendly Islands" comprising the Queendom of Tonga. Niuafou is better known as "Tin Can Island" not because it periodically explodes like a heated tin can (it does), and not because it is constructed like a tin can (it is), but because the 1100 Tongans who live there used to receive their letters in a large tin can thrown overboard by the passing mail boat, trying to avoid the treacherous coral reefs that surround the island. A Polynesian beauty, anxious to read her letter from a dreamy sailor had to grab her canoe and paddle for it. Tin Can Island is unique in that its entire population lives within an active volcano and has for untold generations, in spite of frequent and fearful eruptions.

Bird Pooh Island

Nauru is composed largely of phosphate-rich guano or, as it is better known, bird droppings. This unusual resource has provided Nauruans with one of the highest per capita incomes in the world and has allowed them to build a 51 story skyscraper in Melbourne, the Australian city's tallest building. They also own a first class only airline and a large and growing shipping line. The only problem is that by the 2020's, Naura will be an empty hulk and uninhabitable. But the people of Nauru have several options open to them, including buying another island.

Charles F. Richter

"Many fires burn beneath the earth"
Empedokles (450 B.C.)

Better Not Ask A Scientist "When Will The Earth Explode?" Ask Art Linkletter What Happened When He Asked This Question In An Interview With Charles Richter Of The Richter Scale

When Will We Have Another Earthquake?

The following story first was shared with Buck by Art Linkletter during his visit to the International Swimming Hall of Fame. While Buck was giving Art a deluxe tour of the exhibits, Art entertained Buck with this story which provides a paralleling insight to the great man who devised the method for measuring eruptions:

To   Mr. Buck Dawson

From Art Linkletter

April 11, 1983

Dear Buck:

Thank you for your letter; Briefly, my story
about Richter is, I was interviewing him following
a major earthquake. He was a white haired, small
man with a piping high voice and calm of manner.
Calm, that is, until I asked him a logical question,
namely, when we would have another earthquake. With
that he exploded out of his chair and screamed
"if I am asked that god-damned question once more
I will leave this studio!" Knowing that we were
on tape (live audience) I said "we can cut that
question right out of the tape if you will just sit
down and we can continue the interview." Surprisingly, he subsided and all went smoothly as before.
After the show his companion who had driven him
from Cal Tech apologized for not warning me about
that question, as, with any expert, they are touchy
about direct questions that can not be answered
despite the volume of their knowledge. A lady from
the audience came backstage and asked if this had
all been a "set up" to amuse the audience. I assured
her that what she had just experienced was a true
8.7 eruption on the Richter scale!

All the best to you and your most congeniel colleagues
and thank you for your comments about my swimming,

AL:l

THE DISAPPEARANCE OF THE MAYA MAN POINTING

"Go my people, the land here will be full of salt when the water of this tidal wave recedes." So might have said the Maya priest from his porch atop the pyramid, one of several abandoned mysteriously in the Yucatan peninsula. The date was about 950 A.D. or the equivalent on the Maya calendar. It coincided with Europe's medieval cooling epoch when Lief Erikson discovered North America and the Great Maya civilization to the south disappeared suddenly as if walking into the Bermuda Triangle and leaving all behind. Perhaps this was a migration caused by the same shift in climate that enabled Erickson to get through to Vineland well north of the Yucatan. We know what happened to the Vikings. We don't know why the Maya suddenly abandoned their great civilization.

NUMBER OF HUMANS KILLED BY VOLCANOES										
	10,000	20,000	30,000	40,000	50,000	60,000	70,000	80,000	90,000	100,000
VESUVIUS, Italy 79										
ETNA, Sicily 1169										
KELUIT, Java 1586										
VESUVIUS, Italy 1631										
ETNA, Sicily 1669										
ETNA, Sicily 1693 (plus quakes)										
SKAPTOR JOKEL, Iceland 1783 (plus famine & plague)										
OSEN-OA-TAKE, Japan 1793 (plus tidal wave)										
TAMBORA, Sumbawa 1815										
KRAKATOA, Sundra Strait 1883 (plus tidal wave & quake)										
PELEE, Martinique 1902										
SANTA MARIA, Guatamala 1902										
St. HELENS, Washington, USA 1980										

"Greatest Volcanic Eruptions"

In total numbers killed during all eruptions, Etna is first with a death toll in excess of 350,000. Vesuvius is second. The Java volcanoes and Asamayama, Japan, might top both Etna and Vesuvius if records were available for a longer period. Skaptor Jokel, which erupted in a sparsely populated part of Iceland, can best be measured by the numbers of livestock killed: 200,000 sheep, 28,000 horses and 11,500 cattle. This constituted three-fourths of the island's livestock population.

Recent excavations of an "animal Pompeii" in Nebraska hints that volcanic ash may have been the supernatural force which finally brought down the herbivorous dinosaur after millions of years. By covering his leafy food supply with ash and abruptly changing his climate.

A gas-ash explosive volcano works like champagne

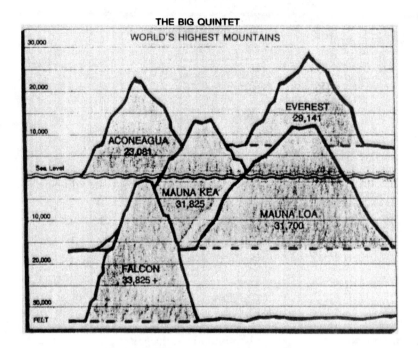

It depends on from where you measure. Aconeagua, Chile, is the highest mountain in the western hemisphere and the highest volcano (if measured above sea level and not from the floor of the ocean). Everest has long been thought to be the world's highest mountain, but Falcon in the South Pacific, is almost 4,000 feet higher yet seldom appears above sea level due to wave action on its cinder cone. Hawaii's Mauna Kea and Mauna Loa are the highest and biggest if measuring the 13,825 feet above sea level and 19,000 from sea level down to their ocean bottom.

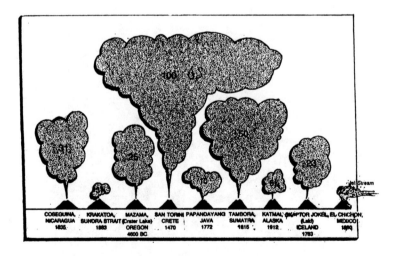

The Biggies – Volume of material ejected (in cubic miles)

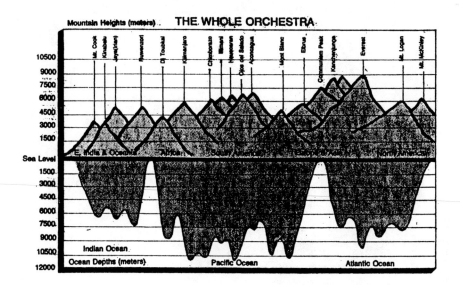

Mountains above and below sea level

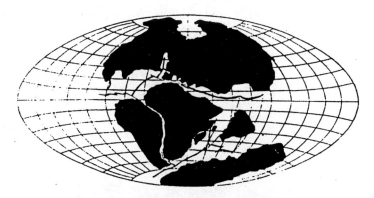

CONTINENTAL DRIFT
Will it come to this and when?

This Continental Drift Theory, like Tectonic Plates, is just that – a theory currently embraced by most scientists. Tomorrow we may have other theories, just as most scientists once believed the earth was flat and Northern Lights came from the midnight sun shining off the ice caps. Many politicized scientists today believe that leaky air conditioners and the burning of fossil fuels can somehow affect global air pollution. It would be far more true to say that termites cause our air pollution since they give off almost twice the CO_2 of all man's combined extravagances and certainly all our burning of fossil fuels.

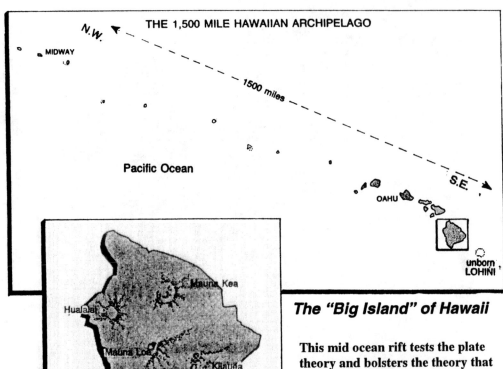

THE 1,500 MILE HAWAIIAN ARCHIPELAGO

N.W.

MIDWAY

1500 miles

Pacific Ocean

S.E.

OAHU

unborn
LOHINI

Mauna Kea

Hualalai

Mauna Loa

Kilauea

The "Big Island" of Hawaii

This mid ocean rift tests the plate
theory and bolsters the theory that
the earth's thin crust on the ocean
bottom is moving over a hot spot.
The 1500 mile chain is all volcanic
but only the big island and the not
yet island of Lohini are active.

The Post Card Volcanoes
World's Most Perfect Cone – Mt. Fuji, Japan

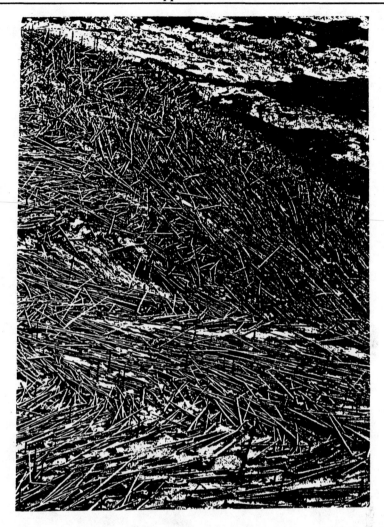

St. Helens: In the Path of Destruction

3.2 billion board feet of timber was blown down or destroyed in a 200-square-mile area – a fatal swath for some who had ventured too near.

A common characteristic of the eruption of both St. Helens in 1980 and the just previous U.S. eruption of Lassen Peak in 1915 were millions of trees blown over and stripped of foliage but not burned as in most other eruptions. The force of these explosions was Peleeon. The blast was great, but the flame was missing. We might have called these the great American tree harvests, clear cutting at its best or worst, depending on which side of the rain forest your moss grows.

The Post Card Volcanoes
World's Most Perfect Cone – Mt. Fuji, Japan

A Close Second – Mt. St. Helens (USA) before the 1980 eruption

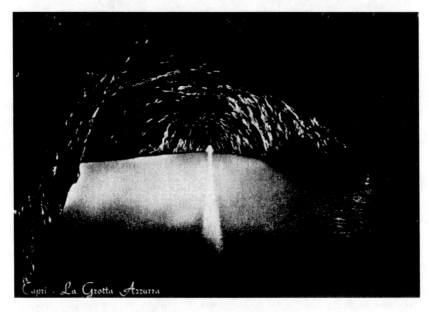

The famed Blue Grotto on Capri is in reality an old lava tunnel

The Devils Tower, Wyoming
Years of erosion have erased the volcanic mound once encasing this extraordinary
mass of igneous rock, the hardened magma core. One of the most conspicuous
features in the Black Hills, the tower rises 600 feet.

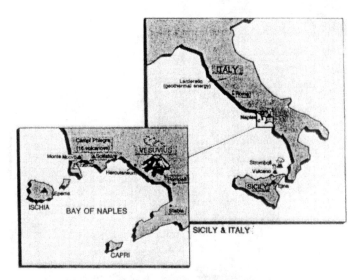

Naples, the capital of the Kingdom of Two Sicilys and Naples Bay, the kingdom of a huge volcano playground.

Harnessing Volcanic Energy
The pioneer Larderello geothermal field just north of Florence, Italy. For heat, electricity, Iceland, Italy and New Zealand point the way by using volcanic steam heat and hot water.

ODE TO VOLCANOES AND THE LIVING EARTH

"Forgive me not! Hate me and
I shall know
Some of love's fire still burns
in your breast!
Forgiveness finds its home in
hearts at rest,
On dead volcanoes only lies the snow."

– Lilla Cabot Perry

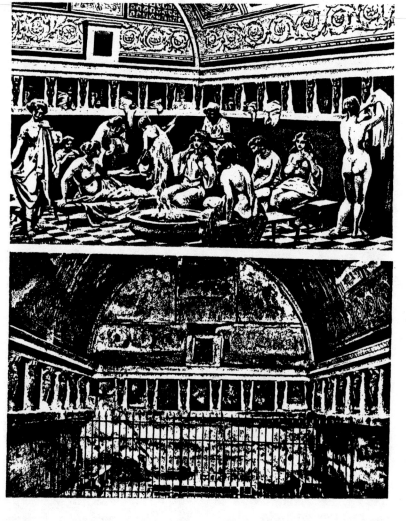

The unknown artist also took liberties on the beauties bathing in Pompeii's famous volcanic waters. The Baths (after excavation) 400 years later didn't attract the same clientele...

"Greatest Volcanic Eruptions"

While St. Helens may be a minor eruption 1/200 the power of Tambora and 1/400 the power of prehistoric Santorini, its 140 billion cubic feet of erupted material still amounts to one ton for every man, woman and child on Earth.

Distance Heard by Human Ear (without hearing device of any kind)				
Volcano	*Location*	*Distance*	*Where Heard*	*Year*
Krakatoa	Sundra Strait	3,000 miles	Rodriguez Is.	1883
Consequina	Nicaragua	1,000 miles	Bogata, Columbia	1835
Tambora	Sumbawa	970 miles	Sumatra	1815
Katmai	Alaska	750 miles	Juneau, Alaska	1912

Numbers of Humans Killed			
Volcano	*Location*	*Number Killed*	*Year*
Etna (plus quake)	Sicily	100,000	1693
Tambora (plus tidal wave)	Sumbawa	56,000	1815
Osen-ga-take (& tidal wave)	Japan	53,000	1793
Pelee	Martinique	40,000	1902
Krakatoa (plus tidal wave and earthquake)	Sundra Strait	36,000	1883
Vesuvius	Italy	25,000	79
Vesuvius	Italy	18,000	1631
Etna	Sicily	17,000	1669
Etna	Sicily	15,000	1169
Skaptor Jokel (famine & plague)	Iceland	10,000	1783
Keluit	Java	10,000	1588
Santa Maria	Guatemala	6,000	1902
St. Helens	Washington USA	59	1980

A Rock By Any Other Name

The rocks exploded out of a volcano are called "blocks" if they are larger than baseballs. The largest "block" on record is a stone 264 by 120 feet, hurled from Asamayama, Japan, in 1783. If these baseball-size pieces are still liquid they are called "clots" or pear-shaped "bombs," depending on how they explode. If they are hard on the outside and still molten inside they are called "breadcrust lava." Small rocks are called "lapilla", which is Latin for "little stone." If the "lapilla" is burned out and porous it becomes "scoria." If it is light gray and floats it is "pumice," which is a frothy form of volcanic glass. Pebbles under pea size are "volcanic ash" unless grainy when they are labeled "volcanic sand." When settled and converted into rock, "lapilla," "clots", and "blocks" combine to become a course substance known as "breccia." Ash and dust become a light porous rock called "tuff."

This volcanic cannonball (bomb) was shot into Whangarei Harbour by the volcano Ngauruhoe, one of three very active volcanoes on the North Island of New Zealand.

Catalogue of Cascade Volcanoes Active in Historic Time or Now Manifesting Thermal Anomalies

From Fire & Ice, The Cascade Volcanoes By Stephen L. Harris

Name of Peak	Dates of Eruptions	Nature and/or Products of Eruptions	Present Thermal Activity
Brokeoff Mountain (Mt. Tehama), CA	–	–	Intense solfataric activity; hot spring fumaroles, steam jet sulphur pots, mud volcanoes, etc.
Lassen Peak, CA	1914-1921	Violent explosions; pyroclastics; lava flows; steam	Small steaming crevice in summit craters; hot spots on north flank
Chaos Crags, CA	1854-1857	Steam	None
Cinder Cone, CA	1850-1851	Lava flow (?) Pyroclastics (?)	None
Mt. Shasta, CA	1786 (?) 1855 (?)	Pumice fragments; steam	Hot sulphur spring summit
Mt. Bailey, Oregon	–	–	Fumaroles; no visible steam
Newberry Crater, Oregon (lies 30 miles east of Cascade Range)	–	–	Hot springs in East lake
Bachelor Butte, Oregon	–	–	Fumaroles on north slope; no visible
Mt. Hood, Oregon	c. 1800 1846 (?); 1854 (?) 1859; 1865 1907	Steam; pyroclastics	Numerous steam vent hot spots surround Crater Rock; emission of hydrogen sulphic
Mt. Saint Helens, Washington	c. 1800; 1831; 1835; 1842-1857 inclusive 1983	Strong explosions; pyroclastics; lava flows (?); steam	Small steam fumarole on north slope, near summit
Mt. Adams, Wash.	–	–	Hydrogen sulphide & small amounts of steam escaping from vents near western summit
Mt. Rainier, Wash.	c. 1820(?); 1841-1843(?); 1854(?); 1879; 1882	Light pumice fall between 1820 and 1854; steam thereafter	Intermittent steam explosions on upper slopes; numerous steam vents and hot rock summit craters.
Mt. Baker, Wash	c. 1820(?); 1843; 1846; 1854-54; 1858; 1859-60; 1963; 1870	Steam, pyroclastics	Intense thermal activity in crater greatly increased after March, 1975 intermittent steam explosions; minor mudflows on east

*"The Moon looks like a golf course compared with what's
up there."*

President Jimmy Carter (USA) at
Press Conference on his Inspection
of the disaster area after St. Helen's
1990 Eruption

*"St. Helens is giving off more exhaust pollution than all the
cars on the road."*

President Ronald Reagan (USA) at Press Conference
to overzealous environmentalists

**Of the Big three since 1980, St. Helens was the cleanest eruption from the standpoint
of polluting gases and strat loading. Both El Chichõn and Mt. Pinatubo caused far
more global air pollution. There are about 30 eruptions a year, each of which top all
man's air pollution.**

The Fire God Vulcan, is all eyes for you...

High in the Andes, Peru, May 1, 1932 where once lava and fire poured forth (2 eyes)–
"An unusually fine photo of two volcanoes made from an expedition plane on flight
over "Valley of the Volcanoes," a valley spotted with hundreds of volcanoes that now
are extinct."

Photo by G.R. Johnson

The largest crater yet discovered off the earth is the huge Olympus Muns on the planet Mars.

The Gold Dust Twins

Mt. Erebus in Antarctica, not only erupts gold dust but has a reception committee of birds dressed in Tuxedos. (official U.S. Navy photo) Maybe this gold dust can be turned into real gold to help offset the huge government debt run up by schemes to save the environment from itself.

Glossary of Volcanic Terms

(Courtesy T.A. Jagaar, Director of the Hawaiian Volcano Observatory)

Aa – rough sprout - lava

Agglomerate – volcanic pudding-stone

Andesite – a light siliceous lava

Anorthite – a basic feldspar

Ash – particles of pulverized rock

Ash Flow – a turbulent mixture of gas and rock fragments

Assimilation – melting up of rocks

Augite – magnesian dark mineral

Basalt – dark heavy lava rich in iron

Basanite – a feldspar basalt

Batholith – deep intrusive magma body underground

Bergschrund – a crevasse at the back of a glacier, formed by melting and the movement of the glacier

Biotite – a dark mica

Block – angular chunk of solid rock

Block and ash flow – variety of pyroclastic flow, turbulent mass of hot fragments

Blocky lava – lava surface that is broken into large angular fragments

Blowhold – miniature crater

Bomb – fragment of molten or semi-molten rock

Breadcrust bomb – eruption bomb with cracked surface

Breccia – rock made of fragments

Burette – graduated glass tube

Caldera – crater of engulfment

Cinder cone – volcanic cone build entirely of loose fragmental material

Clinker – rough fragment of lava on the surface of Aa flows

Cirque – ampitheater-like depression in mountain regions

Composite cone – large volcanic cone constructed of both lava flows and fragmental material

Conduit – the feeding pipe of a volcano

County rock – ancient bedrock

Crater – bowl-shaped hollow, usually at or near the top of a volcano

Cumulo-dome – dome of lava accumulation

Dacite – a quartz-bearing basalt

Detonation – an explosion made by the combustion of gases

Dike – crack filled with lava

Diorite – basic granite rock

Dome – rounded protrusion of lava

Dormant – "sleeping", a volcano which is presently inactive but which may erupt again

Drumlin – gravel dome from under glacier

Ejecta – matter thrown out

Emulsion – a mixture such as dust in gas

Engulfment – the inward collapse of a volcano

Eruption – process by which solid, liquid, and gaseous materials are ejected onto the earth's surface by volcanic activity

Eruption cloud – column of gases, ash and larger rock fragments rising from a crater or other vent

Eruptive vent – the opening through which volcanic material is emitted

Epicenter – place above earthquake source

Exothermic – reaction releasing heat

Fault – rock crack with offset sides

Feldspar – light colored silicate mineral

Fissure – elongated fractures of cracks on the slopes of a volcano or any ground surface

Fumarole – fuming vent

Gabbro – plutonic coarse basaltic rock

Geonomy – science of earth laws

Glowing avalanche – a superheated mass of incandescent ash, blocks, dust and other gas-rich material

Glowing cloud – turbulent mass of gas and dust which rises above the glowing avalanche

Graben – down-sunken fault block

Grano-diorite – between granite and diorite composition

Ground water – underground fresh water body

Hematite – red oxide of iron

Herzberg or Ghyben-Herzberg law – deep ground water body overlies salt water

Holocene Epoch – the 10,000-12,000 year long period of time which has elapsed since the end of the Pleistocent Epoch (Ice Age)

Hornblende – a dark iron-magnesia mineral

Hot avalanche – a glowing avalanche

Horizontal blast – an explosive eruption in which the resultant cloud of hot ash and other material moves laterally rather than upward

Hyalite – glassy transparent hot-spring silica

Hydrothermally altered rock – rock that has been decomposed or otherwise chemically changed by prolonged action of hot steam and/or acidic solutions

Hypersthene – a magnesian dark mineral

Hypomagma – deep gas-charged hot magma

Igneous – fire-melted matter

Ignimbrite – rock consisting of vitric (glassy) ash

Ignisept – dike partition in the globe

Incandescent ash flow – an intensely hot, gas-charged flow of pyroclastic material

Inclusa – matter engulfed

Intrusive – magma that intrudes cavities

Isoseismals – belts of equal earthquake intensity

Isostativ balance – high light land and low heavy sea-bottom

Kame – sand hill left by glacier

Labradorite – a soda-lime feldspar

Laccolith – a lens-shape intrusive body

Lapilli – little stones

Lahar – the Indonesian term for a mudflow

Lava – Magma which has reached the surface through a volcanic eruption

Lava tree mold – the hollow impression left when a tree has been engulfed by a lava flow

Lava tubes – caves or tubes formed inside a lava flow

Leucite – a potash mineral

Lithology – science of rocks

Magma – underground melt that makes lava

Magma chamber – the underground supply house of volcanoes

Magnetic declination – true direction a compass needle points, which periodically
    changes angle. Lava is magnetic

Magnetite – magnetic oxide of iron

Meanders – sinuous curves of a stream

Microearthquakes – extremely small tremors which are perceptible only to sensitive
    scientific instruments

Microlite – microscopic incipient crystal

Monoclinal – tilted in one direction (strata)

Monzonite – a form of crystalline rock

Moraine – gravel heap on a glacier

Neve – mountain snow field

Nuees – Pelee glow clouds moving down rift

Obsidian – siliceous lava glass

Olivine – green siliceous gem mineral

Origina distance – distance to the break underground that causes earthquakes

Pahoehoe – smooth glassy lava surface

Parasitic cone – a (typically small) secondary cone built on the flanks of a larger volcano

Paroxysm – a violently explosive eruption of unusual magnitude

Pegmatite – very coarse granite

Pelean – like Pelee in Martinique

Pele's hair – spun glass lava

Phreatic – eruptive steamy of ground water origin

Pliocene Epoch – period of geologic time immediately preceding the Pleistocene and
    lasting from about 7,000,000 to 2 or 3,000,000 years before the present

Pisolitic – mud raindrops size of peas are pisolites

Plagioclase – the soda-lime feldspar group

Planetesimal theory – that the earth grew from assembled cold meteors

Plinian or paroxysmal – eruptive by violent steam-blasts

Plug – solidified lava that fills the conduit or "throat" of a volcano

Plug dome – the steep-sided, rounded mound formed when viscous lava wells up into a crater and is too stiff to flow away

Plutonic – deep fire-made rock like granite

Post-miocene – period after middle Tertiary

Preliminary phase – first motion of earthquake recorded on seismograph

Pumice – solidified form of rock-glass which was highly charged with gas when blown from a crater

Pyroclastics – the Greek work for "fire-broken" referring to fragmented volcanic rock

Pyroclastic flow – a volcanic flow of hot gas and fragmental material

Pyroxene – dark mineral in lava

Quaternary – the geologic period that includes both the Pleistocene and Holocene Eoch

Rhyolite – excessively siliceous lava

Rift belt – an eruptive cracked zone

Schist – ancient mica rock

Scoria – porous ejected lava fragment

Scree – gravel slide slope

Siesmograph – instrument which detects and records earthquakes, including those too weak to be perceptible to most persons

Self-heating lava – heating by escape of dissolved gas

Selvage – glassy edge to igneous rock section

Shield volcano – a broad, very gently sloping volcano built almost exclusively of lava flows

Sill – intrusive lava between strata

Sinter – a hot spring accretion

Silicic lava – lava rich in silica (over 65%) and having a relatively low melting point (850 degrees Centigrade)

Sofatara – sulphrous hot place

Sp. gr. – specific gravity

Spiracle – lava spire built up

Stratovolcano – a volcano composed of both lava flows and fragmental (pyroclastic) material

Tailings – rock refuse from a mining crusher

Talus – a gravel slope

Tangi – a Maori funeral

Tectonic – structural in the earth crust

Teleseism – distant earthquake seismogram

Tephra – terms used by Aristotle to describe air-born pyroclastic ("fire-broken") material which has been erupted by a volcano

Tephrite – a peculiar feldspar basalt

Tertiary – the geologic age before the glacial period

Tilt – tipping of the ground

Tree-mold – a hold in a lava flow created by lava forming the hollow impression of a tree trunk

Tree-well – the cylindrical hole in a lava flow caused by the carbonization or decay of a tree trunk which had been engulfed in the flow

Tridymite – a crystal form of silica

Tuff – hardened volcanic dust or fragments

Tumescence – underground lava expanding the land

Vent - opening in the earth's surface through which volcanic material is ejected

Vesicular – porous with gas bubbles

Viterous – glassy from quick solidifying

Volcanicity – underground volcanic condition of a country

Volute – cloud puff

Vulcan – Roman god of fire and the forge, after whom volcanoes are named

Vulcanian eruption – a type of eruption characterized by violent explosions which send dark cauliflower clouds of ash into the air

Vitric – term describing volcanic material consisting chiefly of glassy matter, such as vitric ash which is at least 75% glass

Water-table – subterranean top surface of the ground-water

Welded tuff – rock composed of fine-grained material which was hot enough when emplaced to weld or fuse together

INDEX